This book is from

the kitchen library of

_____

_____

ALSO BY ART GINSBURG, MR. FOOD®

Mr. Food®
One Pot,
One Meal

Art Ginsburg
Mr. Food®

WILLIAM MORROW AND COMPANY, INC.

NEW YORK

It is the policy of William Morrow and Company, Inc., and its imprints and affiliates, recognizing the importance of preserving what has been written, to print the books we publish on acid-free paper, and we exert our best efforts to that end.

Library of Congress Cataloging-in-Publication Data

Ginsburg, Art.
    Mr. Food®, one pot, one meal / Art Ginsburg.
        p.   cm.
    Includes index.
    ISBN 0-688-14577-9
    1. Casserole cookery.
TX693.G57 1997
641.8'21—dc21   97-590
                                                                                 CIP

Printed in the United States of America

First Edition

1   2   3   4   5   6   7   8   9   10

BOOK DESIGN BY MICHAEL MENDELSOHN OF MM DESIGN 2000, INC.

Dedicated to

All the hardworking people who
rush home every night to put a homemade meal
on the table for their families.

Hooray for you!

You've been asking for this,
so here's *your* book!

Acknowledgments

When I told my staff that we were going to create a cookbook based completely on one-pot recipes, the room was full of smiles . . . especially from our fabulous dishwasher, Al. He was more excited than anyone, 'cause he loves the idea of having just one pot to wash for each recipe! (And so will you!)

Now, any good recipe needs a bunch of elements to come together successfully, and the same goes for putting together this book. I thank my incredible kitchen staff of Patty, Janice, Cheryl, Joan, and Karen, who tested and retested potful after skilletful after bowlful. A special thanks goes to Joe, Laura, and Helayne for their attention to all the details of planning and documenting our work in the kitchen and through the various stages of production. And I can't forget to express my appreciation to the rest of my staff, who all practically have second jobs as food testers in our kitchen: Steve, Chuck, Ethel, Tom, Chet, Carol, Marilyn, Beth, and Alice. Thanks for your input, guys!

My friends at William Morrow—Al, Paul, Zach, Lisa, Deborah, Anne, Michael, Jackie, and Richard—continue to pull everything together and make my books happen. I thank you, and also my agent, Bill, and my designer, Michael, for continuing to help me come up with winners.

Caryl and Howard keep stirring the pot to allow all the right flavors to "marry," this time resulting in yet another book full of tasty recipes and loads of fun in the kitchen.

Acknowledgments

My devoted readers and viewers are great! All of you make it possible for me to do this work that I love. Thanks for allowing me into your homes—both in my books and on my TV show.

I'm also grateful to the following companies for their support of my work:

Moore Farming, Inc., growers and packers of
    Salad Savoy®

National Presto Industries, Inc., makers of
    Presto® pressure cookers

Rival Manufacturing Company, makers of the
    Rival® Crock-Pot®

Tefal S.A. France, makers of T-Fal® nonstick cookware

Tryson House®, makers of flavor mists

Villa Valenti Classic Sauce Company

Contents

Introduction

Here we are, closing in on the twenty-first century, and our lives are busier and more complicated than ever! It used to be that people had more time for cooking—or so it seemed. I sure remember the days when there was almost always something roasting in my mom's oven while there was a stovetop full of pots and pans and a dinner table full of platters. It's impossible to forget the taste of comfort that Mom cooked into every bite . . . *or* the sink full of dishes that she'd have facing her *after* dinner!

After all these years, is there a better way? How do we enjoy hearty, tasty meals today with all the juggling we have to do to manage our busy, complicated lives? Well, sometimes we don't have to cook at all! With all the great take-out selections available to us these days, it's possible to pick up one or two ready-to-eat items, or an entire home-cooked–tasting meal. And, if we plan ahead, then we can take advantage of the home-style offerings in the growing freezer sections of our supermarkets. Of course, buying prepared foods is helpful, but it isn't always the best way to keep food costs down.

So what if you still want to make your own home-cooked meals in your limited available time? What if I told you it's possible to do it without giving up hours and hours for preparation and cleanup? It sounds as if it must be magic, but it's not. Stick with me and I'll show you just how easy it can be to prepare entire meals, each in just one pot or pan.

When the pressure is really on, and time is ticking away,

Introduction

turn to the good old standby that's better than ever—the pressure cooker. If you're my age or older, you'll remember them from years ago, except that today's pressure cookers are improved and safer than ever. And what cooking time they save! Pressure cookers cut cooking time by 30% to 75%. You have to see it to believe it! So try some goodies like Chunky Beef and Bean Chili (page 68), Quick Beef Stew (page 67), and even Stuffed Cornish Hens (page 78) and Lemon-Steamed Swordfish (page 79)! Pressure cookers are super . . . they can change your life!

While you were digging in your cabinet, looking for your pressure cooker, you may have come across your slow cooker or your wok. It's time to bring them out and dust them off, 'cause they're going to become your helpers now, too! Slow cookers let you prepare dinner the night before, or in the morning, so that you can come home to a hot and ready dinner that evening. And with either an electric wok or one that you use on the stovetop, you can cook up a fresh, satisfying dinner in under ten minutes!

Sure, you can use slow cookers and woks to make your family's old favorites, but why not score some big points with the gang by whipping up new dishes like Chicken 'n' Wild Rice (page 51), No-Fuss Beefy Minestrone Soup (page 53), Shrimp Special Fried Rice (page 92), and Sweet-and-Sour Pork (page 87)? You'll wonder how you ever got along without these dishes!

Skillets are a must-have in every kitchen. They're so versatile! And after you try easy meals like Jazzy Jambalaya (page 127), Philly Chicken Subs (page 131), and Chinese Chicken Roll-ups (page 130), you'll see why skillets are such a popular choice.

Then there are casseroles. When we think of comfort and good times, we think of casseroles. With their steaming-hot

Introduction

goodness in every forkful, casseroles bring back memories of great times. So get ready to try my chapter brimming with favorites of yesterday and today like Beef Burgundy Casserole (page 138) and Tuna Rice Casserole (page 149).

Now, let's not forget about roasts and bakes. You know, luscious meat and poultry surrounded by flavorful potatoes and veggies? Our slow-cooking oven meals like Lemon Rosemary Chicken (page 167) and Crown Roast of Lamb (page 160) go together in minutes, then the oven does the rest!

Along with all the meals I've mentioned, there are plenty more that'll please you and your gang. From hearty big-pot meals like Harvest Veal Stew (page 22) and Fish Chowder (page 15) to refreshing Taco Steak Salad (page 37) and Caribbean Chicken Salad (page 35), there are lots of ways to come up a winner every time. And I haven't even mentioned the new pasta dishes that are here! When everybody tastes your Spicy Rigatoni (page 102) and Thai Chicken Pasta (page 107), they won't believe you made it all in one pot!

Now, when we think of one-pot cooking, I guess things made on baking sheets don't really come to mind. But I rounded up so many one-pan goodies like Vegetable Pockets (page 178) and Oven-Baked Reubens (page 181) that I had to include a chapter of those types of meals, too. I'm sure you'll be glad I did!

Okay, now you're ready to go! Whether you're having company over, or just wondering what you can throw together at the last minute for a complete meal for your family, you've got plenty of choices here. It'll probably take you longer to *decide* what to make than it will to *make* what you choose! I hope I've helped. Have fun!

A Note About Packaged Foods

Packaged food sizes may vary by brand. Generally, the sizes indicated in these recipes are average sizes. If you can't find the exact package size listed in the ingredients, whatever package is closest in size will usually do the trick.

The Big Pot

Simmering Soups, Stews, and More

When we think of one-pot meals, the first thing most of us think of is that big soup pot simmering away on the stove, full of all the makings for a satisfying meal. I bet you make them all the time, too—your favorite stews and throw-together soups that you "beef up" to make hearty enough to be a complete meal.

Well, those are the kinds of recipes I've got in here. And no, these aren't all dishes that need to cook for hours and hours. Some are simply mixed and heated. And the ones that *do* require more cooking time *don't* require more preparation time . . . 'cause the range does all the work!

Now, before you say "Soup's on!"—here are a few soup pot pointers:

- Make sure you start with a large enough soup pot. (There's nothing worse than having to clean up soup or stew that's splattered all over the stovetop!)

- Since all ranges vary, yours may be cooler or hotter than average. Keep an eye on the heat so your meal won't burn.

- Use sturdy, long-handled spoons for stirring so you can keep your fingers and hands from being burned.

- Rest it—your spoon, that is. Place your spoon and other cooking utensils on a spoon rest or small heat-proof plate on or beside your stovetop. It'll make for easier cleanup.

1

The Big Pot

Simmering Soups, Stews, and More

3

Shepherd's Pie Soup

4 to 6 servings

How could you go wrong making these great tastes into a soup?!

1 pound ground lamb or beef
5 cups water
2 cans (10½ ounces each)
    condensed beef broth
1 package (16 ounces) frozen
    diced potatoes
1 package (16 ounces) frozen
    mixed vegetables

1 teaspoon onion powder
1½ teaspoons salt
½ teaspoon black pepper
2 cups instant mashed potato
    flakes

In a 6-quart soup pot, brown the ground meat over medium-high heat for 8 to 10 minutes. Add the remaining ingredients except the potato flakes and bring to a boil. Reduce the heat to medium-low and simmer for 12 to 15 minutes, or until the vegetables are tender. Stir in the potato flakes and cook for 5 to 7 minutes, or until thickened. Serve immediately.

Beef Barley Soup

Did you know how quickly you can make one of everybody's all-time favorite homemade soups? Try it and see! (I know it'll be gone in no time!)

1 pound beef cubed steak, cut
    into ¾-inch chunks
1 tablespoon all-purpose flour
½ teaspoon black pepper
1 tablespoon olive oil
8 cups water

6 beef bouillon cubes
½ cup pearled barley
3 medium-sized carrots,
    shredded
1 large onion, diced
1 celery stalk, diced

Sprinkle the beef with the flour and pepper. In a 6-quart soup pot, heat the oil over high heat, then add the beef and brown on all sides for 6 to 7 minutes. Add the remaining ingredients and bring to a boil, then reduce the heat to medium and cook for 45 to 50 minutes, or until the barley is tender.

Scotch Broth

Don't let the name fool you—this is far from a traditional clear broth. It's a lamb and vegetable stew that's full of chunky goodness!

2 pounds lamb stew meat, trimmed and cut into ¾-inch chunks
2 medium-sized onions, cut into wedges
4 medium-sized celery stalks, sliced
6 cups water
8 small turnips (about 1¼ pounds), peeled and quartered

6 medium-sized carrots, cut into ½-inch chunks
2 garlic cloves
1 bay leaf
1 tablespoon salt
½ cup pearled barley

In a 6-quart soup pot, brown the lamb, onions, and celery over medium-high heat for 8 to 10 minutes. Add the remaining ingredients except the barley and bring to a boil. Add the barley, cover, and reduce the heat to low; simmer for 55 to 60 minutes, or until the barley is tender. **Be sure to remove the bay leaf before serving.**

Split Pea and Ham Soup

4 to 6 servings

If you're like me, a big bowl of pea soup is satisfying enough to be a whole stick-to-your-ribs meal. And with the ham that's in this one, you're in for a filling treat in every spoonful!

8 cups water
1 pound fully cooked boneless ham, cut into ½-inch chunks
1 package (24 ounces) dry green split peas
4 large potatoes, peeled and cut into 1-inch chunks
2 medium-sized onions, chopped
2 medium-sized carrots, cut into ½-inch chunks
2 celery stalks, cut into ½-inch chunks
2 chicken bouillon cubes
1 teaspoon salt
1 teaspoon black pepper

In a 6-quart soup pot, combine all the ingredients over medium-high heat and bring to a boil. Reduce the heat to low, cover, and simmer for 50 to 60 minutes, or until the vegetables are tender.

NOTE: You can use leftover ham in this, or buy it right from the deli case. Don't forget to refrigerate any leftovers! And if the soup is too thick after it has been chilled, just stir in a little water when rewarming it to achieve the desired consistency.

Hearty Bean Soup

5 to 7 servings

Break out a loaf of hearty rye bread and get ready for some good old-fashioned dunking!

3 cups water
One 2-pound fully cooked
   center-cut ham steak, cut
   into 1-inch chunks
4 cans (15½ ounces each)
   Great Northern beans,
   undrained

5 medium-sized potatoes,
   peeled and diced
1 large onion, chopped
1 celery stalk, chopped
1 medium-sized carrot,
   chopped
½ teaspoon black pepper

In a 6-quart soup pot, combine all the ingredients over medium-high heat and bring to a boil. Reduce the heat to low, cover, and simmer for 45 to 50 minutes, or until the potatoes are fork-tender.

Turkey Noodle Soup

No more taking a back seat to chicken noodle soup! Uh-uh! You're gonna be gobblin' up your own homemade turkey noodle soup in no time.

8 cups water
2 turkey thighs or drumsticks
   (about 3 pounds total)
2 medium-sized onions,
   coarsely chopped
3 medium-sized carrots, cut
   into 1-inch chunks

2 celery stalks, cut into 1-inch
   chunks
2 teaspoons salt
½ teaspoon black pepper
8 ounces medium egg noodles
1 package (16 ounces)
   frozen corn

In an 8-quart soup pot, combine all the ingredients except the noodles and corn. Bring to a boil over high heat, then reduce the heat to low, cover, and simmer for about 1½ hours, or until the turkey is fork-tender and cooked through. Carefully remove the turkey from the pot; remove and discard the bones and skin, then cut the meat into chunks. Meanwhile, increase the heat under the soup to high and bring to a boil; add the noodles to the pot and cook for 5 minutes. Return the turkey meat to the pot, add the corn, and cook for 4 to 5 minutes, or until the noodles are tender and the corn is thoroughly heated. Serve immediately.

Chicken and Broccoli Cheese Soup

6 to 8 servings

It's all right here—your favorite Cheddar cheese soup studded with chunks of chicken and broccoli. Mmm, mmm!

½ cup (1 stick) butter
1 cup all-purpose flour
11 cups water
3 chicken bouillon cubes
2 pounds boneless, skinless
   chicken breasts, cut into
   ½-inch chunks

2 bunches broccoli, trimmed
   and chopped
1½ teaspoons salt
1 teaspoon black pepper
1 cup (½ pint) heavy cream
3 cups (12 ounces) shredded
   Cheddar cheese

In a 6-quart soup pot, melt the butter over medium heat. Add the flour, stirring constantly until a thick paste is formed. Remove to a small bowl and set aside. In the same pot, combine the water, bouillon cubes, chicken, broccoli, salt, and pepper. Bring to a boil over high heat, then reduce the heat to medium-low and simmer for 45 minutes, or until the broccoli is tender. Stir in the flour mixture a little at a time until the soup is thickened. Simmer for 5 minutes, then reduce the heat to low and slowly stir in the heavy cream, mixing well. Add the cheese 1 cup at a time, mixing well after each addition until the cheese melts. Serve immediately.

New York, New York Clam Chowder

3 to 4 servings

Some people call this Manhattan clam chowder, but I like to call it New York, New York, 'cause it's twice as good as the others!

2 tablespoons vegetable oil
1 large onion, chopped
2 celery stalks, chopped
2 medium-sized carrots,
    chopped
5 medium-sized potatoes,
    peeled and diced

2 cans (14½ ounces each)
    diced tomatoes, undrained
2 cans (10 ounces each) baby
    clams, undrained
1 bottle (8 ounces) clam juice
2 tablespoons real bacon bits
1 teaspoon dried thyme

In a 6-quart soup pot, heat the oil over medium-high heat until hot but not smoking. Add the onion, celery, and carrots and sauté for 5 to 7 minutes, or until the onions are tender, stirring frequently. Add the remaining ingredients and bring to a boil. Reduce the heat to low and simmer for 50 to 55 minutes, or until the potatoes are fork-tender.

Fresh Catch Soup

4 to 6 servings

If you like clam chowder, wait till you taste this seafood soup challenger that's ready to spin your ladle in a new direction!

5 cups water
1 can (28 ounces) crushed
   tomatoes
2 pounds fresh or frozen
   white-fleshed fish fillets,
   such as cod, haddock, or
   whiting, thawed if frozen,
   cut into 1-inch pieces

1 package (16 ounces) frozen
   mixed vegetables (broccoli,
   cauliflower, and carrots)
1¼ cups uncooked long-
   grain rice
1 bay leaf
2 teaspoons salt
½ teaspoon black pepper

In a 6-quart soup pot, combine all the ingredients over high heat and mix well. Bring to a boil, then reduce the heat to low, cover, and simmer for 20 to 25 minutes, or until the rice is tender. **Be sure to remove the bay leaf before serving.**

Souped-up Crab Bisque

4 to 6 servings

According to the dictionary, a bisque is a thick cream soup. According to my family, it's a tasty meal all in one bowl.

2 tablespoons butter
1 large onion, diced
1 plum tomato, diced
1 celery stalk, diced
1 garlic clove, minced
½ teaspoon paprika
2 tablespoons all-purpose
   flour

2 cans (14½ ounces each)
   ready-to-use chicken broth
3 medium-sized potatoes,
   peeled and diced
4 cups (1 quart) heavy cream
3 cans (6 ounces each)
   crabmeat, drained and
   flaked

In a 6-quart soup pot, melt the butter over high heat; sauté the onion, tomato, celery, garlic, and paprika for 5 to 6 minutes, or until the onion is tender. Stir in the flour until well mixed. Stir in the chicken broth and potatoes and cook for 10 minutes. Reduce the heat to low; stir in the cream, then the crabmeat. Simmer for 15 to 18 minutes, or until the soup is hot throughout, stirring occasionally. Do not allow to boil.

NOTE: For more color, I like to serve this garnished with sliced scallions.

Fish Chowder

4 to 6 servings

No need to seek out the best chowder recipe at the seashore, 'cause it's right here, spoonful after warming spoonful.

6 cups (1½ quarts) milk
1 package (10 ounces) frozen corn
1 package (9 ounces) frozen peas
2 pounds fresh or frozen white-fleshed fish fillets, such as cod, haddock, or whiting, thawed if frozen, cut into 2-inch pieces

1 tablespoon dried thyme
1½ teaspoons onion powder
1 teaspoon dried basil
1½ teaspoons salt
1 teaspoon black pepper
1½ cups instant mashed potato flakes

In a 6-quart soup pot, combine all the ingredients except the potato flakes over medium-high heat. Bring to a boil, then reduce the heat to low and simmer for 8 to 10 minutes. Stir in the potato flakes, then simmer for 3 to 5 minutes, or until thickened. Serve immediately.

NOTE: If the soup gets too thick, don't hesitate to add a little more milk to thin it.

Zesty Cioppino

4 to 6 servings

A San Francisco treat that's just as welcome at home as it is on Fisherman's Wharf.

½ pound fresh mushrooms, sliced

2 medium-sized onions, thinly sliced

4 garlic cloves, minced

1 can (28 ounces) whole Italian-style tomatoes, undrained

1 cup dry white wine

1 teaspoon black pepper

2 pounds red snapper or cod fillets, cut into 2-inch chunks

1 pound bay scallops

1 pound large shrimp, peeled and deveined, but tails left on

Spray a 6-quart soup pot with nonstick vegetable spray and heat over high heat. Add the mushrooms, onions, and garlic and cook for 4 to 6 minutes, or until the vegetables are tender, stirring often. Stir in the tomatoes, wine, and pepper. Bring to a boil, then reduce the heat to low, cover, and simmer for 20 minutes. Remove the lid and increase the heat to high. Bring to a boil and add the fish, scallops, and shrimp. Cook for 8 to 10 minutes, or until the fish flakes easily with a fork and the shrimp are pink and cooked through, stirring occasionally.

NOTE: For a true taste of San Francisco, serve this with sourdough bread.

Seafood Ragout

3 to 4 servings

Calling all seafood lovers! Grab a spoon and a package of oyster crackers, 'cause this one's what fishermen call "good eatin"!

2 tablespoons butter
1 cup sliced fresh mushrooms
1 medium-sized onion, chopped
2 cups (1 pint) half-and-half
2 cans (8 ounces each) oysters, drained and liquid reserved
1 can (12 ounces) tuna in water, drained and liquid reserved

1 cup uncooked long- or whole-grain rice
1 package (10 ounces) frozen cooked shrimp, thawed
2 tablespoons chopped fresh parsley

In a 6-quart soup pot, melt the butter over medium-high heat and sauté the mushrooms and onion for 6 to 7 minutes, or until the onion is golden. Add the half-and-half and the reserved liquid from the oysters and tuna. Bring to a boil, then add the rice, cover, and reduce the heat to low. Simmer for 25 to 30 minutes, or until the rice is tender. Stir in the oysters, tuna, and shrimp and simmer for 6 to 8 minutes, or until heated through. Sprinkle with the parsley just before serving.

NOTE: You can substitute whole or chopped clams for the oysters, if you prefer.

Frogmore Stew

4 to 6 servings

In Beaufort, South Carolina, where this dish hails from, folks just spread newspaper on the table and dump this stew right on it. Then it's every person for himself as everybody grabs and eats what he wants. It's a perfect "serve yourself" dinner.

8 cups water
2 tablespoons seafood seasoning
½ teaspoon salt
¼ teaspoon cayenne pepper
1 pound kielbasa sausage, cut into 2-inch pieces
6 medium-sized potatoes, cut in half
6 medium-sized onions, peeled and cut in half
3 ears corn, cut into 3-inch pieces
1 pound large shrimp, unpeeled

In a 6-quart soup pot, combine the water, seafood seasoning, salt, and cayenne pepper. Bring to a boil over high heat and add the sausage, potatoes, onions, and corn. Cook for 15 to 20 minutes, or until the potatoes are fork-tender. Add the shrimp and cook for 2 to 3 minutes, or until the shrimp are pink and cooked through. Strain the stew and serve immediately, along with bowls of the broth for dunking.

Almost Gumbo

4 to 6 servings

The authentic taste of the bayou, without all the authentic work!

1 pound smoked sausage, cut lengthwise in half, then crosswise into ½-inch slices
4 cups water
1 can (14½ ounces) stewed tomatoes
1 package (10 ounces) frozen cut okra, thawed and drained

2 teaspoons dried thyme
1 teaspoon garlic powder
½ cup uncooked long- or whole-grain rice
¼ cup dry red wine
1 tablespoon hot pepper sauce

In a 6-quart soup pot, combine the sausage, water, tomatoes, okra, thyme, and garlic powder. Bring to a boil over medium heat, then reduce the heat to low and add the remaining ingredients. Simmer for 20 to 25 minutes, or until the rice is tender, stirring occasionally.

NOTE: Add a pound of cooked peeled shrimp 5 minutes before serving, if desired.

Farmer's Stew

4 to 6 servings

Whether you've had a hectic day on the farm or at another job, you're in for a hearty meal at sunset with this stew.

3 tablespoons olive oil
1 to 1½ pounds boneless, skinless chicken breasts, cut into 1-inch chunks
2 medium-sized onions, chopped
8 garlic cloves, coarsely chopped, divided
6 plum tomatoes, cut into 1-inch chunks
3 medium-sized zucchini, cut into 1-inch chunks
2 medium-sized red bell peppers, cut into 1-inch chunks
½ cup chopped fresh parsley, divided
1 tablespoon dried basil
2 teaspoons dried oregano
1½ teaspoons salt
½ teaspoon black pepper
2 cans (15 ounces each) whole potatoes, drained
Finely grated peel of 1 lemon

In a 6-quart soup pot, heat the olive oil over high heat. Add the chicken, onions, and three quarters of the chopped garlic. Cook for 8 to 10 minutes, or until the chicken is browned on all sides, stirring frequently. Reduce the heat to medium and add the tomatoes, zucchini, red peppers, ¼ cup parsley, the basil, oregano, salt, and black pepper. Cover and cook for 10 minutes, then add the potatoes, lemon peel, and the remaining chopped garlic and ¼ cup chopped parsley. Stir until thoroughly mixed, then cover and cook for 5 to 7 minutes, or until the potatoes are warmed through. Serve immediately.

Italian Veal Stew

4 to 6 servings

Ladle out the goodness into soup bowls and listen for all the cries of "Bene! Molto bene!" (Italian for "It's good! It's really good!")

3 tablespoons vegetable oil
2 pounds veal stew meat,
    trimmed and cut into
    1-inch chunks
1 large onion, chopped
3 celery stalks, chopped
2 garlic cloves, finely chopped
1 can (28 ounces) whole
    Italian-style tomatoes, cut
    into quarters, undrained

2 pounds potatoes, cut into
    large chunks
½ cup dry white wine
½ cup chopped fresh parsley
1 teaspoon dried rosemary
1½ teaspoons salt
½ teaspoon black pepper

In a 6-quart soup pot, heat the oil over medium-high heat. Add the veal and brown on all sides for 5 to 8 minutes. Add the onion, celery, and garlic and sauté for 3 to 5 minutes, or until the vegetables are tender, stirring frequently. Stir in the remaining ingredients and bring to a boil. Reduce the heat to low, cover, and simmer for 1 to 1½ hours, or until the veal is fork-tender.

Harvest Veal Stew

4 to 5 servings

This stew sure brings back lots of fond memories of cool autumn days in Upstate New York. The only thing missing is the apple picking and the hot spiced cider.

2 pounds veal stew meat, trimmed and cut into 1-inch chunks

2 cans (16 ounces each) vegetarian baked beans

1 package (10 ounces) frozen cut carrots

1 package (8 ounces) mixed dried fruit

1 large onion, chopped

¼ cup water

3 tablespoons dark brown sugar

1 tablespoon white vinegar

1 tablespoon lemon juice

½ teaspoon salt

1 can (29 ounces) yams, drained

In a 6-quart soup pot that has been coated with nonstick vegetable spray, brown the veal over high heat for 7 to 8 minutes. Reduce the heat to medium and add the remaining ingredients except the yams; mix well. Bring to a boil, then cover and reduce the heat to low; simmer for 40 to 45 minutes, stirring occasionally. Gently stir in the yams, then cover and simmer for 15 minutes, or until the yams are thoroughly heated.

Welcome-Home Pot

4 to 6 servings

When you've got this simmering on the stove, the gang's gonna come home from work and school to an aroma that says, "Welcome home!"

1½ cups water
4 pounds beef short ribs
3 medium-sized red potatoes,
    quartered
2 medium-sized onions,
    chopped
4 medium-sized carrots, cut
    into 1-inch chunks

⅓ cup pearled barley
2 cans (16 ounces each)
    vegetarian baked beans
½ teaspoon salt
¼ teaspoon black pepper

In a 6-quart soup pot, combine the water, short ribs, potatoes, onions, carrots, and barley; bring to a boil over high heat. Reduce the heat to low, cover, and simmer for 3½ to 4 hours, or until the meat is fork-tender. Skim off the fat, then stir in the beans, salt, and pepper; cover and simmer for 40 minutes. Serve immediately.

Spiced Beef and Rice

3 to 4 servings

Lots of beef, rice, veggies, and spices, all served up in no time . . .

2 tablespoons vegetable oil
1½ pounds boneless beef top
    sirloin steak, cut into
    ¼" × 3" strips
1 small green bell pepper,
    finely chopped
1 small onion, finely chopped
1 can (14½ ounces) Mexican-
    style stewed tomatoes

1 package (10 ounces) frozen
    peas, thawed
1 cup water
¾ cup uncooked long-
    or whole-grain rice
2 teaspoons garlic powder
2 teaspoons chili powder
¾ teaspoon salt
⅛ teaspoon black pepper

In a 6-quart soup pot, heat the oil over high heat. Add the steak, bell pepper, and onion and sauté for 3 to 5 minutes, or until the beef is browned. Stir in the remaining ingredients and bring to a boil. Reduce the heat to low, cover, and simmer for 30 to 35 minutes, or until the beef is tender and the rice is cooked.

Chunky Vegetable and Beef Chili

4 to 6 servings

So often we hear people arguing over which chili is the best—ones with beef, just beans, with vegetables. . . . Well, here's a way to compromise that should satisfy everybody, with *no* compromise in taste!

2 pounds ground beef
1 medium-sized onion, chopped
1 can (28 ounces) crushed tomatoes
1 can (16 ounces) pinto beans, undrained
½ cup water

2 tablespoons honey
2 large zucchini, coarsely chopped
2 medium-sized red bell peppers, coarsely chopped
3 tablespoons chili powder
1½ teaspoons salt
¾ teaspoon black pepper

In a 6-quart soup pot, brown the beef and onion over medium-high heat for 5 to 6 minutes, or until no pink remains in the beef; drain off the excess liquid. Add the remaining ingredients; mix well, cover, and bring to a boil. Reduce the heat to low and simmer for 45 to 50 minutes, or until the vegetables are tender, stirring occasionally.

Mexican Twist

Don't be so quick to get out your blue suede shoes and poodle skirt! This twist is served up on the kitchen table, not the dance floor.

1 pound ground beef
1 large onion, chopped
4 cups water
1 can (15¼ ounces) whole
    kernel corn, drained

1 can (14½ ounces) diced
    tomatoes, undrained
2 envelopes (1¼ ounces each)
    dry taco seasoning mix
8 ounces spiral pasta

In a 6-quart soup pot, brown the ground beef and onion over high heat for 8 to 10 minutes, until no pink remains in the beef and the onion is tender. Add the remaining ingredients except the pasta; mix well. Bring to a boil, then stir in the pasta. Reduce the heat to low, cover, and simmer for 15 to 18 minutes, or until the pasta is tender.

Stuffed Bell Peppers

6 servings

When the dinner bell rings and you're ready to serve, just remember that you were saved by the bell . . . pepper, I mean!

1 can (29 ounces) tomato
    sauce
1 cup water
1 teaspoon garlic powder
1 teaspoon salt
½ teaspoon black pepper

1 pound ground beef
1 cup uncooked instant rice
1 small onion, chopped
6 large green bell peppers,
    washed, tops removed,
    and seeded

In a 6-quart soup pot, combine the tomato sauce, water, garlic powder, salt, and black pepper; mix well. Remove 1 cup of the mixture to a large bowl. Add the ground beef, rice, and onion to the bowl; mix well. Stuff each bell pepper with an equal amount of the mixture and place in the soup pot. Spoon some sauce from the pot over the peppers. Cover and cook for 55 to 60 minutes over low heat, or until no pink remains in the meat and the rice is tender. Spoon the sauce over the peppers and serve.

Ham 'n' Dumplings

6 to 8 servings

Apples are the perfect go-along for almost any pork dinner, especially a smoked ham. And in this dish that originated with the Pennsylvania Dutch, we get an extra treat, 'cause the apples and pork are nestled in the same pot with puffy homemade dumplings. Believe it or not, that apple and pork combo is even better now!

8 cups water
One 2½-pound fully cooked
   semi-boneless ham
2 packages (6 ounces each)
   dried apples

3 cups biscuit baking mix
1 cup milk

In an 8-quart soup pot, combine the water, ham, and apples over medium-high heat and bring to a boil. Reduce the heat to low, cover, and simmer for 20 minutes. In a medium-sized bowl, combine the baking mix with the milk just until moistened. Uncover the soup pot and carefully drop the batter by heaping tablespoonfuls into the pot, making 8 dumplings. Cook, uncovered, for 10 minutes. Cover and cook for 18 to 20 more minutes, or until the dumplings are fluffy and doubled in size.

NOTE: Dried apples can be found by the raisins, prunes, and other dried fruit in your supermarket.

Chicken and Dumplings

4 to 6 servings

All right, I'll admit that it wasn't too long ago that I had my first taste of chicken and dumplings. And, let me tell you, it didn't take long before I had them again . . . and then again!

2 tablespoons vegetable oil
1 chicken (2½ to 3 pounds),
    cut into 8 pieces
3 cans (14½ ounces each)
    ready-to-use chicken broth
2 cups water, divided
3 carrots, cut into ½-inch
    slices
3 celery stalks, cut into ½-inch
    slices

2 medium-sized onions, cut
    into wedges
1 teaspoon salt
1 teaspoon black pepper
½ cup all-purpose flour
3 cups biscuit baking mix
1 cup milk

In a 6-quart soup pot, heat the oil over medium-high heat and cook the chicken for 8 to 10 minutes, until browned on all sides, turning halfway through the cooking. Drain off the fat and add the broth, 1¼ cups water, the carrots, celery, onions, salt, and pepper. Bring to a boil, then reduce the heat to low and simmer for 30 to 35 minutes, or until the vegetables are fork-tender. In a small bowl, combine the flour and the remaining ¾ cup water; mix well. Pour into the chicken mixture and stir until thickened. In a medium-sized bowl, combine the baking mix with the milk just until moistened. Carefully drop the batter by heaping tablespoonfuls into the simmering broth, making 8 dumplings. Cook, uncovered, for 10 minutes. Cover and cook for 12 to 15 more minutes, or until the dumplings are fluffy and doubled in size. Serve immediately.

Old-fashioned Chicken

3 to 4 servings

Here's a dish we rarely taste anymore, and I don't know why. After all, it takes us back to Mom's kitchen, without all the fuss of preparing it like she did.

2 tablespoons olive oil
½ teaspoon salt
8 chicken thighs or drumsticks
    (about 2 pounds)
1 medium-sized onion,
    chopped
2 cans (14 to 16 ounces each)
    cannellini beans (white
    kidney beans), drained
2 cans (15 ounces each) whole
    potatoes, drained

1 can (28 ounces) whole
    tomatoes, chopped, juice
    reserved
2 tablespoons tomato paste
1 tablespoon dried tarragon
2 teaspoons garlic powder
¼ teaspoon crushed red
    pepper

In a 6-quart soup pot, heat the olive oil over medium heat. Sprinkle the salt over the chicken and cook for 20 minutes, until browned on all sides, turning several times. Add the onion and sauté for about 2 minutes; drain off the fat. Add the remaining ingredients to the pot; mix well. Bring to a boil, then reduce the heat to low and simmer for 20 minutes, until the chicken is tender and no pink remains.

NOTE: You can use any type of bean here in place of the cannellini beans . . . you know, pinto beans, garbanzo beans (chick peas), or black-eyed peas.

The Salad Bowl

A Toss-up

Salad as a meal? You betcha! I mean, how many times have you sat down to start a meal with a nice big salad that you just ate and ate until, before you knew it, it filled you right up? Of course, that bread and butter you ate helped, too! Why, you probably didn't even feel like eating your main course after that, did you? Well, why not go ahead and make yourself a hearty salad that you *plan* on having as your whole meal?

There are quite a few salad treats in here. But before you get ready to toss or layer your first main-course salad, keep in mind these few tips:

- Make salads in or on glass, wooden, or stainless steel bowls or platters; the acids in many dressings can stain plastic or react with certain metals.

- Be sure to use a bowl or platter that's large enough to allow plenty of room for tossing.

- Don't be afraid to experiment. Add or subtract items from my recipes to suit your tastes. Remember, these are *your* salads.

- Get away from your same old routine. Be adventurous! Mix and match different greens. Wake up your regular salads by using a variety of textures and colors. Don't feel guilty about using bagged premixed salads, either. They're really convenient and can add excitement to your meal.

- Add hot grilled or steamed meat, chicken, or veggies to a chilled salad; the temperature contrast makes for a nice change of pace.

- When it's time to "get dressed," do so moderately. Don't drown your salad—you're supposed to taste the fresh ingredients, not just the dressing.

The Salad Bowl

A Toss-up

Cobb Salad

4 to 6 servings

A classic, no matter how you arrange it. And it tastes just as great at home as it does in any restaurant . . . maybe better, 'cause you'll be sure to put in all your favorites!

1½ pounds boneless, skinless chicken breasts, cut into ½-inch chunks
½ teaspoon salt
¼ teaspoon black pepper
1 medium-sized head iceberg lettuce, cut into bite-sized pieces
½ cup real bacon bits
1 large tomato, coarsely chopped
1 avocado, peeled, pitted, and chopped
3 hard-boiled eggs, chopped
4 scallions, thinly sliced
1 package (4 ounces) crumbled blue cheese

Sprinkle the chicken with the salt and pepper. In a large skillet that has been coated with nonstick vegetable spray, brown the chicken over medium-high heat for 5 to 6 minutes, stirring occasionally. Remove the chicken and set aside to cool slightly. Meanwhile, arrange the lettuce on a large serving platter. Place the cooked chicken in the center of the lettuce. Place the bacon bits in a row on one side of the chicken. Place the tomatoes in a row next to the bacon bits and the chopped avocado in a row next to them. Place the chopped eggs in a row on the other side of the chicken. Place the chopped scallions in a row next to the eggs and the crumbled blue cheese in a row next to them. Serve immediately.

NOTE: Serve with a creamy salad dressing like ranch or Thousand Island.

Caribbean Chicken Salad

When you're feelin' hot, hot, hot, wouldn't it be nice to have a taste of the tropics in a whole-meal salad?

1 cup sour cream
3 tablespoons confectioners' sugar
2 cups diced cooked chicken
2 firm bananas, cut into ½-inch slices
3 celery stalks, chopped
1 can (20 ounces) pineapple chunks, drained

1 can (11 ounces) mandarin oranges, drained
½ cup flaked coconut (see Note)
½ cup cashew pieces
⅛ teaspoon black pepper
1 medium-sized head iceberg lettuce, shredded

In a large bowl, combine the sour cream and confectioners' sugar; mix well. Stir in the remaining ingredients except the lettuce; toss until thoroughly mixed. Place the shredded lettuce on a serving platter or divide among 4 to 6 serving plates; top with the chicken mixture. Serve immediately.

NOTE: To enhance the flavor of the coconut, spread it on a baking sheet and toast in a 350°F. oven for 2 to 3 minutes, or until golden brown.

Asian Chicken Salad

6 to 8 servings

When most of us think about cabbage and salad, we think of coleslaw. Well, how 'bout making that team into something really special?

2 tablespoons sesame oil
½ cup sesame seeds
4 garlic cloves, minced
2 pounds boneless, skinless
    chicken breasts, cut into
    ½-inch chunks
¾ cup vegetable oil

½ cup sugar
¼ cup soy sauce
¼ cup white vinegar
1 head Napa (Chinese)
    cabbage, cut into bite-sized
    pieces
¼ pound snow peas, trimmed

In a large skillet, heat the sesame oil over medium heat; sauté the sesame seeds and garlic for 2 to 3 minutes, or until the sesame seeds are golden brown. Add the chicken, vegetable oil, sugar, soy sauce, and vinegar and cook for 4 to 5 minutes, or until no pink remains in the chicken. Meanwhile, place the cabbage and snow peas in a large bowl or on a serving platter. Top with the chicken mixture and toss until well coated. Serve immediately.

NOTE: For a little added color and flavor, add a can of drained mandarin oranges to the salad.

Taco Steak Salad

Even if it isn't fiesta time, this main-dish salad will get everybody in a partying mood!

2 tablespoons dry taco
   seasoning mix
One 1½-pound beef flank
   steak
2 tablespoons butter
1 medium-sized head iceberg
   lettuce, cut into bite-sized
   pieces
1 medium-sized tomato,
   chopped
1 can (15 ounces) red kidney
   beans, rinsed and drained
1 cup (4 ounces) shredded
   Monterey Jack cheese
¾ cup salsa (see Note)
½ cup sour cream

Rub the taco seasoning evenly over the entire surface of the steak. In a large skillet, melt the butter over medium-high heat and cook the steak for 14 to 16 minutes for medium, or to desired doneness, turning halfway through the cooking. Remove the steak to a plate and allow to cool slightly. Meanwhile, on a large serving platter, layer the lettuce, tomato, kidney beans, and cheese. In a small bowl, combine the salsa and sour cream; mix well and spoon over the salad. Cut the steak across the grain into ¼-inch slices and place on top of the salad. Serve immediately.

NOTE: The spiciness of the dressing depends on the intensity of the salsa you use. If you want a really spicy dressing, use hot salsa. If you don't want it too spicy, use a mild one.

Warm Beef and Penne Salad

4 to 6 servings

Warm salads have become really popular, and this one's a sure hit 'cause of the creamy, rich flavors. Oh, yeah—then there's the added zip of tongue-tingling horseradish. . . . That makes it unforgettable!

1 pound penne pasta
¼ cup olive oil, divided
1 large red onion, cut into thin wedges
1 pound boneless beef chuck steak, cut into ¼-inch strips

1 cup mayonnaise
½ cup sour cream
3 tablespoons prepared horseradish, drained
½ teaspoon salt
½ teaspoon black pepper
4 plum tomatoes, chopped

In a 6-quart soup pot, prepare the pasta according to the package directions; drain, rinse, drain again, and set aside in the colander. In the same pot, heat 1 tablespoon oil over medium-high heat and sauté the onions and steak for 4 to 5 minutes, or until the steak is browned, stirring occasionally. Remove from the heat. In a large bowl, combine the mayonnaise, sour cream, horseradish, salt, pepper, and the remaining 3 tablespoons olive oil. Stir until well combined, then add the beef mixture, pasta, and tomatoes; toss until well coated. Serve warm.

NOTE: I serve this as a warm salad, but some people say they like it even better after it has chilled for a couple of hours. The choice is yours!

Little Italy Antipasto

4 to 6 servings

There are lots of cities across America that have their own versions of New York's Little Italy—you know, a place where you can get a fantastic Italian meal. Well, how 'bout giving this genuine Italian antipasto a try? In no time, your house will be known as the local kitchen that serves the most authentic Italian salad!

1 medium-sized head iceberg lettuce, cut into bite-sized pieces

¼ pound thinly sliced deli ham, cut into ½-inch strips

¼ pound thinly sliced Genoa or other hard salami, cut into quarters

½ pound mozzarella cheese, cut into 1-inch chunks

2 medium-sized tomatoes, cut into chunks

1 jar (6 ounces) marinated artichoke hearts, drained and quartered

1 jar (7 ounces) roasted peppers, drained and cut into ½-inch strips

¾ cup peperoncini (about 12), drained

1½ cups extra-large pitted black olives (about 20), drained

DRESSING

½ cup olive oil

½ cup red wine vinegar

¾ teaspoon salt

¼ teaspoon white pepper

Place the lettuce on a large platter. Layer the remaining salad ingredients over the lettuce. In a small bowl, combine the dressing ingredients; mix well. Pour half of the dressing over the salad and add more to individual servings as needed.

NOTE: Sometimes I like to add some dried oregano or basil to the dressing for even more of that Little Italy flavor.

Chef's Salad

4 to 6 servings

Just because this is called Chef's Salad doesn't mean that everybody else can't make it . . . uh-uh! This version will knock your socks off, and you won't believe how simple it is for anybody—chef or not—to put together!

1 large head iceberg lettuce, cut into bite-sized pieces
1 small red onion, sliced
1 small cucumber, sliced
2 celery stalks, chopped
6 radishes, sliced
½ pound thinly sliced deli turkey, cut into julienne strips
½ pound thinly sliced deli ham, cut into julienne strips
¼ pound thinly sliced Swiss cheese, cut into julienne strips
3 hard-boiled eggs, cut into wedges
2 medium-sized tomatoes, cut into wedges
1 cup croutons

Place the lettuce, onion, cucumber, celery, and radishes in a large serving bowl; toss lightly. Arrange the turkey, ham, and cheese in rows over the lettuce and top with the eggs, tomatoes, and croutons.

NOTE: Serve with a creamy Italian dressing or even your favorite low-fat dressing.

Salad Niçoise

4 to 6 servings

The French are known for their great food, and this salad is modeled after the Nice (pronounced Nees) original. Chock-full of chunks of tuna, red potatoes, hard-boiled eggs, green beans, and black olives, and drizzled with red wine vinaigrette, it's loaded with ooh-là-là!

1 medium-sized head iceberg lettuce, cut into bite-sized pieces

½ pound green beans, trimmed, cooked, and chilled

5 medium-sized red potatoes, cooked, cut into 1-inch chunks, and chilled

6 hard-boiled eggs, cut into wedges and chilled

1 can (12 ounces) tuna, drained and flaked

1 can (3¼ ounces) whole pitted black olives, drained

1 bottle (16 ounces) red wine vinaigrette dressing

In a large serving bowl, layer the lettuce, green beans, potatoes, and hard-boiled eggs. Top with the tuna and olives. Drizzle with the dressing as desired and serve immediately.

Salmon Caesar Salad

4 servings

We all love a good, crisp Caesar salad. And this one's a little different from the usual, 'cause it's topped with broiled salmon. I know you're gonna have a new favorite now!

4 salmon fillets (about
    1 pound total)
1 envelope (1.2 ounces) dry
    Caesar salad dressing mix,
    divided
½ cup olive oil
¼ cup white vinegar

1 can (2 ounces) anchovies,
    drained and finely
    chopped
1 large head romaine lettuce,
    cut into bite-sized pieces
1 package (6 ounces) croutons
¼ cup grated Parmesan cheese

Preheat the broiler. Place the salmon on a broiler pan or a rimmed baking sheet that has been coated with nonstick vegetable spray; rub the top of each fillet with 1 teaspoon dressing mix. Broil for 6 to 8 minutes, or until the fish is lightly browned and flakes easily with a fork. Meanwhile, in a large bowl, combine the oil, vinegar, anchovies, and the remaining dressing mix; mix well. Add the lettuce, croutons, and Parmesan cheese and toss until thoroughly coated. Divide the lettuce mixture evenly among 4 serving plates and top each with a salmon fillet. Serve immediately.

NOTE: The salmon can be served warm right out of the broiler, or it can be cooked ahead of time, chilled, and served cold.

Creamy Shrimp Caesar Salad

4 to 6 servings

I know, I've said it before and I'll say it again: I love Caesar salad! And since I believe that expression about variety being the spice of life, I try Caesar salad all different ways. This one sure gets my attention . . . again and again!

2 cans (15 ounces each) garbanzo beans (chick peas), drained
1 can (14 ounces) artichoke hearts, drained and quartered
1 bottle (16 ounces) creamy Caesar salad dressing
1 package (10 ounces) frozen cooked shrimp, thawed and drained

1 can (3¼ ounces) whole pitted black olives, drained
6 radishes, quartered
1 teaspoon dried oregano
1 medium-sized head romaine lettuce, cut into bite-sized pieces

In a large bowl, combine all the ingredients except the lettuce; toss until well mixed. Place the lettuce on a serving platter and top with the shrimp mixture. Serve immediately.

Pasta Crab Salad

4 to 6 servings

You want something quick and easy, but it has to be tasty and satis-fying, too, right? If you're a fan of seafood and pasta salads, then give this crab salad a spin. You'll be crawling back for more!

1 pound cheese tortellini (see Note)	2 celery stalks, chopped
	1½ cups mayonnaise
1 pound imitation crabmeat, flaked	1 tablespoon lemon juice
	1½ teaspoons salt
1 medium-sized red bell pepper, finely chopped	½ teaspoon black pepper
	3 tablespoons heavy cream

Cook the tortellini according to the package directions; drain, rinse, and drain again. Set aside to cool in the colan-der. In a large bowl, combine the cooled tortellini and the remaining ingredients except the cream. Mix until thor-oughly combined, then stir in the cream. Cover and chill for at least 2 hours before serving.

NOTE: You can use fresh, frozen, or dried tortellini—or even use meat-filled tortellini for added flavor.

Seashell Salad

4 to 6 servings

Everybody loves the roar of the ocean—and the roar of the crowd. So why not have the best of both with this salad that's sure to make waves?!

1 pound small seashell pasta
1 can (20 ounces) pineapple
   tidbits in heavy syrup,
   drained
1 medium-sized red onion,
   finely chopped
1½ cups mayonnaise

¼ cup honey
½ teaspoon paprika
1 teaspoon salt
½ teaspoon black pepper
1 package (12 ounces) frozen
   cooked large shrimp,
   thawed and drained

Cook the pasta according to the package directions; drain, rinse, drain again, and set aside in the colander to cool. In a large bowl, combine the remaining ingredients except the shrimp; mix well. Add the shrimp and cooled pasta and toss to combine. Cover and chill for at least 2 hours before serving.

The Slow Cooker

Ready-and-Waiting Meals

I'll admit it—I was one of those countless people who had an electric slow cooker (known to most by the brand name Crock-Pot®) buried in my kitchen cabinet. I hadn't touched it in years. Boy, was that ever a mistake!

I got it out when I started working on this book, and the more I cooked with it, the more I found out how handy it is. You just put your food in it, cover it, set the timer, and you're done! You can go off to work or out for the day and know that you're going to come home to dinner all ready and waiting in one pot. All it takes is a little planning so that you can prepare your meal ahead of time. It cooks while you're off working or playing.

I've often been asked how it can be safe to let food cook in a slow cooker all day, but research shows that it's okay as long as food reaches 200°F. and continues to cook at a temperature consistently at or above 200°F. So follow these few basic steps to see just how fast you can learn to slow-cook:

- Slow cookers come in various sizes. I recommend a size large enough to accommodate the many different recipes you'll be making in it.

- I prefer a slow cooker with a removable crock (the inside glass container) so that a dish can be put together the night before and refrigerated until I start cooking it the following morning. (This works great if you don't have

47

any extra time in the morning; it makes cleanup after the meal a breeze, too!)

- **Before using a slow cooker, read the manufacturer's care and cleaning instructions carefully. Do not immerse the electrical cooking elements in water.**

- **Be safe! Always start with cold food items and do not allow frozen food to thaw in a slow cooker before being cooked in it.**

- Do not add extra liquid to the slow cooker, as is done in some traditional methods of cooking. Moisture is retained in slow cookers and doesn't cook away.

- **The key to success in slow-cooking is keeping the slow cooker covered!** That keeps in the moisture *and* the cooking heat.

- If you need your dish to be ready sooner than the recommended cooking time and your recipe calls for using low heat, you can often cook your dish on high heat, since each hour on high heat is equal to 2 to 3 hours on low heat.

The Slow Cooker

Ready-and-Waiting Meals

All-Day Macaroni and Cheese

4 to 6 servings

I don't think I've ever had a creamier version of macaroni and cheese. And since my grandchildren tasted it, this has become a regular at our house!

8 ounces elbow macaroni, cooked and drained
1 can (12 ounces) evaporated milk
1½ cups milk
2 eggs

4 cups (16 ounces) shredded sharp Cheddar cheese, divided
1 teaspoon salt
½ teaspoon black pepper

Place the cooked macaroni in a 3½-quart (or larger) slow cooker that has been coated with nonstick vegetable spray. Add the remaining ingredients except 1 cup of the cheese; mix well. Sprinkle with the remaining 1 cup cheese, then cover and cook on the low setting for 5 to 6 hours, or until the mixture is firm and golden around the edges. Do not remove the cover or stir until the macaroni has finished cooking.

Chicken 'n' Wild Rice

4 to 6 servings

They'll go wild for this one, 'cause after the flavors get the whole day to blend together, your finished dish is creamy and melt-in-your-mouth delicious!

2 pounds boneless, skinless chicken breasts, cut into 1-inch cubes

2 packages (6 ounces each) wild and long-grain converted rice mix with seasoning packets

2½ cups water

1 can (10¾ ounces) condensed broccoli cheese soup

½ cup (1 stick) butter, melted

2 medium-sized onions, finely chopped

1 cup broccoli florets

½ pound processed cheese spread, cut into ½-inch cubes

In a 3½-quart (or larger) slow cooker, combine all the ingredients; mix well. Cover and cook on the low setting for 6 to 10 hours.

Turkey Breast with Cranberry Stuffing

4 to 6 servings

Okay, here it is—the way to have a turkey dinner with all the trimmings without going to all the trouble of stuffing a whole turkey and making all the side dishes separately. Once you try this, you may never make it any other way!

1 package (8 ounces) stuffing cubes
½ cup hot water
2 tablespoons butter, softened
1 small onion, chopped
1 can (4 ounces) sliced mushrooms, drained
¼ cup sweetened dried cranberries

One 3-pound boneless turkey breast
¼ teaspoon dried basil
½ teaspoon salt
½ teaspoon black pepper
6 medium-sized carrots, cut into 1-inch chunks

Coat a 3½-quart (or larger) slow cooker with nonstick vegetable spray. Put the stuffing cubes in the cooker and add the water, butter, onion, mushrooms, and cranberries; mix well. Sprinkle the turkey breast with the basil, salt, and pepper. Place the turkey over the stuffing mixture, then place the carrots around the turkey. Cover and cook on the low setting for 6 to 7 hours. Remove the turkey to a cutting board and slice. Place the carrots on a serving platter. Stir the stuffing until thoroughly mixed and allow to sit for 5 minutes. Spoon onto the platter with the carrots and top with the sliced turkey.

No-Fuss Beefy Minestrone Soup

8 to 10 servings

I love to serve steaming-hot homemade soup, and this is one that doesn't have to be constantly watched over. It's so hearty that it can double as a whole meal!

1¼ pounds beef stew meat, cut into ¾-inch chunks

3 cans (14½ ounces each) ready-to-use beef broth

1 can (28 ounces) crushed tomatoes

1 can (15 ounces) red kidney beans, undrained

1 can (15 ounces) garbanzo beans (chick peas), undrained

1 package (10 ounces) frozen chopped spinach, thawed, drained, and squeezed dry

2 medium-sized zucchini, coarsely chopped

1 medium-sized onion, chopped

1 teaspoon garlic powder

1 teaspoon salt

½ teaspoon black pepper

1 cup uncooked elbow macaroni

In a 6-quart slow cooker, combine all the ingredients except the macaroni; mix well. Cover and cook on the low setting for 6 to 8 hours, or until the meat is tender. Add the macaroni and cook on the high setting for 30 minutes. Serve immediately, or reduce to the low setting until ready to serve.

Easy-Cook Pot Roast

4 to 6 servings

The name pretty much says it all . . . except that this is one of the best meals around!

4 medium-sized potatoes,
    peeled and quartered
3 medium-sized carrots, cut
    into 2-inch chunks
1 medium-sized onion, sliced
¼ cup all-purpose flour
2 teaspoons salt
½ teaspoon black pepper

One 3-pound beef eye of the
    round roast, trimmed
1 can (4 ounces) mushrooms,
    drained
1 can (10¼ ounces) beef gravy
1½ teaspoons browning and
    seasoning sauce

Place the potatoes, carrots, and onion in a 6-quart slow cooker. In a shallow dish, combine the flour, salt, and pepper. Coat the beef on all sides with the flour mixture and place over the vegetables in the slow cooker. Place the mushrooms over the roast, then pour the gravy over the top. Cover and cook on the low setting for 7 to 8 hours. One hour before removing the roast from the slow cooker, remove the cover and turn the roast over. When it has finished cooking, remove the roast to a cutting board. Add the browning and seasoning sauce to the slow cooker and stir gently. Slice the roast and serve with the vegetables and sauce.

Make-Ahead Hungarian Beef Stew

4 to 6 servings

If you're in a stew about what to fix for dinner, here's one that you can toss together in the morning for a warm, satisfying meal when you get home from your busy day!

3 medium-sized potatoes, peeled and cut into 1-inch chunks

2 large onions, cut into large chunks

5 medium-sized carrots, cut into 1-inch chunks

1 package (10 ounces) frozen lima beans, thawed

2 pounds beef stew meat or chuck roast, cut into 1½-inch chunks

1 can (14½ ounces) diced tomatoes, undrained

½ cup ready-to-use beef broth

2 garlic cloves, minced

2 tablespoons paprika

1½ teaspoons salt

½ cup instant mashed potato flakes

1 cup sour cream

In a 3½-quart (or larger) slow cooker, combine the potatoes, onions, carrots, and lima beans; mix well. In a large bowl, combine the meat, tomatoes, broth, garlic, paprika, and salt; place over the vegetables in the slow cooker. Cover and cook on the low setting for 8 to 10 hours, or until the meat is fork-tender. Stir in the potato flakes until well mixed and the stew has thickened. Just before serving, stir in the sour cream.

NOTE: Although this is a hearty meal by itself, serving it over warm buttered egg noodles creates a real Hungarian delight!

Slow-Cooked Meat Loaf and Potatoes

6 to 8 servings

Have you ever thought of making meat loaf in a slow cooker? It's a worry-free way to make the family favorite. (But it's so good that, sorry, I can't promise there'll be leftovers for cold meat loaf sandwiches!)

2 medium-sized potatoes, peeled and cut into 1-inch cubes

2 pounds ground beef (see Note)

½ pound hot Italian turkey sausage, casings removed

1 large onion, finely chopped

1½ cups ketchup, divided

¾ cup crushed butter-flavored crackers

2 eggs

2 teaspoons salt

⅓ cup firmly packed light brown sugar

½ teaspoon prepared yellow mustard

Place the potatoes in a 3½-quart (or larger) slow cooker. In a large bowl, combine the beef, sausage, onion, ¾ cup ketchup, the cracker crumbs, eggs, and salt; mix well. Place over the potatoes and pat down to form a loaf. In the same bowl, combine the brown sugar, mustard, and the remaining ¾ cup ketchup; mix well. Spread over the top of the loaf, cover, and cook on the low setting for 6 to 10 hours. Drain off the excess liquid and serve.

NOTE: I recommend using lean ground beef to minimize the amount of fat.

Pasta and Meatballs

3 to 4 servings

The possibilities are endless when we cook our meatballs and pasta at the same time. (You'll love the easy cleanup, too!)

1 can (28 ounces) tomato purée

1 can (15 ounces) tomato sauce

1 can (4 ounces) sliced mushrooms, drained and coarsely chopped

1 medium-sized onion, finely chopped

2 garlic cloves, minced

½ teaspoon dried oregano

¼ teaspoon dried basil

1 teaspoon salt, divided

1 pound ground beef

¼ cup seasoned bread crumbs

1 egg

½ pound angel hair (capellini) pasta, broken into 4-inch pieces

In a 3½-quart (or larger) slow cooker, combine the tomato purée, tomato sauce, mushrooms, onion, garlic, oregano, basil, and ½ teaspoon salt; mix well. In a medium-sized bowl, combine the ground beef, bread crumbs, egg, and the remaining ½ teaspoon salt; mix well and form into 1-inch balls. Gently place the meatballs in the sauce; do not mix. Cover and cook on the low setting for 5 to 8 hours. Remove the cover and add the angel hair pasta; do not stir. Replace the cover and increase the setting to high. Cook for 1 hour, then stir and serve.

NOTE: If you want to mellow the taste of the tomato sauce, add a teaspoon of sugar along with the tomato purée, or add a diced medium-sized carrot. (That adds sweetness *and* nice texture!)

Oh-So-Tender Osso Buco

4 servings

My family knows that I have a weakness for Osso Buco. I can't help it! It reminds me of the veal dishes my mom used to make, where the meat would be so tender from hours of cooking that it'd just fall right off the bone. This is a great way to get those same long-cooked flavors, without much fuss.

2 cans (14½ ounces each) whole potatoes, drained
1 can (14½ ounces) sliced carrots, drained
1 large tomato, coarsely chopped
2 tablespoons lemon juice
1 tablespoon chopped fresh parsley
1 teaspoon garlic powder
½ teaspoon salt
½ teaspoon black pepper
4 veal shanks (3 to 4 pounds total)
1 envelope (1 ounce) dry onion soup mix
1¼ cups water, divided
¼ cup dry red wine
¼ cup cornstarch

In a 3½-quart (or larger) slow cooker, lightly toss together the potatoes, carrots, tomato, lemon juice, parsley, garlic powder, salt, and pepper. Place the veal shanks on top, sprinkle with the onion soup mix, and add 1 cup water. Cover and cook for 7 to 9 hours on the low setting. Remove the veal shanks to a serving platter and cover to keep warm. With the slow cooker still on the low setting, stir the red wine into the sauce and vegetable mixture. In a small bowl, combine the remaining ¼ cup water and the cornstarch. Stir into the sauce and vegetable mixture until thickened. Pour over the veal shanks and serve immediately.

Garden-"Stuffed" Pork Chops

4 servings

Here's a shortcut to the yummy flavors of stuffed pork chops that'll taste as if it's right out of the garden . . . and before you know it, you'll be right out of the kitchen!

4 pork loin chops (1 to 1½ pounds total), ¾ inch thick
¼ teaspoon salt
⅛ teaspoon black pepper
1 can (15 ounces) tomato sauce, divided

1 large green bell pepper, chopped
1 small onion, chopped
1½ cups herb stuffing cubes
½ teaspoon dried rosemary

Place the pork chops in a 3½-quart (or larger) slow cooker. Sprinkle with the salt and black pepper. Pour half of the tomato sauce over the chops. In a large bowl, combine the remaining ingredients, including the remaining tomato sauce; mix well. Spoon over the pork chops, cover, and cook on the low setting for 7 to 9 hours.

Cranberry Pork Roast

4 to 6 servings

Most of us think of cranberries only around holiday time, but they've got a taste that we can love anytime. So go ahead and give 'em a new combination that explodes with cranberry flavor.

4 medium-sized potatoes, peeled and cut into 1-inch chunks

One 3-pound boneless center-cut pork loin roast, rolled and tied

1 can (16 ounces) whole-berry cranberry sauce

1 can (5.5 ounces) apricot nectar

1 cup pearl onions

½ cup coarsely chopped dried apricots

½ cup sugar

1 teaspoon dry mustard

¼ teaspoon crushed red pepper

Place the potatoes in a 3½-quart (or larger) slow cooker, then place the roast over the potatoes. In a large bowl, combine the remaining ingredients; mix well and pour over the roast. Cover and cook on the low setting for 5 to 6 hours. Remove the roast to a cutting board and thinly slice. Serve with the potatoes and sauce.

Chinese Cashew Tuna

4 to 6 servings

Wait till you hear all the raves you get for turning a plain can of tuna into crunchy magic. They'll be nuts about it (*and you*)!

1 can (10¾ ounces) condensed cream of mushroom soup
1 can (14 ounces) bean sprouts, drained
1 can (6 ounces) tuna, drained and flaked
1 small onion, finely chopped
3 celery stalks, diced
½ of a medium-sized red bell pepper, finely chopped
1 tablespoon soy sauce
1 package (6 ounces) frozen snow peas, thawed
1 cup roasted cashew halves
1 package (5 ounces) chow mein noodles

In a 3½-quart (or larger) slow cooker, combine the soup, bean sprouts, tuna, onion, celery, red pepper, and soy sauce; mix well. Cover and cook on the low setting for 5 to 9 hours. Remove the cover and stir in the snow peas and cashew halves; cook for 3 to 4 minutes, until warmed through. Serve over the chow mein noodles.

The Pressure Cooker

Quick Cooking Under Pressure

If I told you that you could cook your food in half to three quarters of the time of traditional cooking methods and still enjoy rich, slow-cooked taste, wouldn't you be interested? Let me introduce you to an easy kitchen tool that makes that possible: the pressure cooker!

Unlike the pressure cookers of yesterday, today's pressure cookers are quite safe, and they're much more user-friendly. Of course, **before you do any cooking with one, you've got to read the manufacturer's directions carefully and be sure you understand them.**

The idea of pressure cooking is just what its name says: cooking under pressure. The steam that's produced by cooking this way creates a hot, moist environment for cooking food. Again, **I can't stress enough the importance of thoroughly reading and following the pressure-cooker manufacturer's directions.**

And before you get started, you should also know the following:

- Pressure cookers come in various sizes—I recommend a size large enough to accommodate the many different recipes you'll be making in it. It's generally better to go with one that's bigger than you think you'll need, since you should never fill a pressure cooker more than two-thirds full. (Many items increase in size during cooking.)

63

- Did you know you get a bonus with a pressure cooker? It can be used simply as a traditional stockpot (using it without pressure). So it comes in handy when you just need a large cooking pot, and also when you're making pressure-cooking recipes that call for browning meats or veggies before beginning to cook with pressure.
- **There must always be some liquid used when cooking under pressure. Never begin cooking without liquid!**
- If you prefer cooking a roast or veggies without them sitting in liquid, place the food on the cooking rack, keeping it out of the juices on the pot bottom.
- Place the ingredients in the pressure cooker as directed in the recipe. Secure the top and place the rocker cap on the vent. Place over the specified heat. When the regulator begins to gently rock back and forth, lower the heat according to the recipe instructions; the regulator should continue to rock gently. **This is when to begin timing the cooking.**
- Cook for the instructed cooking time, then cool the entire pressure cooker one of two ways: either by removing it from the heat and simply allowing the pressure to drop slowly naturally, or by carefully placing the cooker in the sink and running cold water over it. (This is called the quick-release method.)
- Once the cooker is cooled and the safety lock releases on its own, it is safe to remove the pressure regulator and unlock the lid.
- If additional cooking is needed, replace the lid and repeat the pressure cooking process for the necessary amount of time.

Now that you've read my tips carefully, reread your instruction book, then try Heat-'em-Up Chili (page 71) or Flavor-Packed Brunswick Stew (page 77). They're quick, tasty ways to get familiar with your pressure cooker!

The Pressure Cooker

Quick Cooking Under Pressure

Stovetop Rump Roast

4 to 6 servings

Now you can make a rump roast in just about an hour! Oh, yes—you want to know about the taste . . . ? As if it's been roasting all day!

One 4- to 5-pound beef rump
    roast
2 teaspoons salt
1½ teaspoons black pepper
¼ cup olive oil
4 large onions, coarsely
    chopped

1½ cups water, divided
6 large potatoes, peeled and
    cut in half
6 large carrots, cut into 3-inch
    chunks
¼ cup all-purpose flour

Sprinkle the roast with the salt and pepper. Heat the oil in a 6-quart pressure cooker over high heat. Add the roast and brown on all sides, uncovered, for about 10 minutes. Add the onions and 1 cup water. Lock the lid in place and bring to full pressure over high heat. When the pressure regulator begins to rock, reduce the heat to medium and cook for 60 minutes. Cool the cooker at once by placing under cold running water until steam no longer escapes from the vent and the pressure is completely reduced. Remove the lid; place the roast on a cutting board and cover to keep warm. Add the potatoes and carrots to the pressure cooker. Lock the lid in place and bring to full pressure over high heat. When the pressure regulator begins to rock, reduce the heat to medium and cook for 5 minutes. Cool the cooker at once, as above. Remove the lid and place the vegetables on a serving platter. In a small bowl, whisk together the remaining ½ cup water and the flour until smooth. Stir into the drippings in the cooker and heat, uncovered, over medium-high heat for 5 to 6 minutes, or until thickened. Slice the roast and serve with the vegetables and sauce.

Quick Beef Stew

4 to 6 servings

You'll have no beef with this one, 'cause all the pressure's in the pot (*not* on you)! Try it for a fast, hearty helping of down-home good flavor!

2 tablespoons vegetable oil
2½ pounds boneless beef
    chuck roast or steak, cut
    into 1-inch cubes
2 teaspoons salt
1 teaspoon black pepper
6 medium-sized potatoes
    (about 2 pounds), peeled
    and cut into quarters
6 medium-sized carrots, cut
    into 1-inch chunks

2 medium-sized onions, cut
    into wedges
1 can (14½ ounces) ready-to-
    use beef broth
1½ cups water, divided
¼ cup all-purpose flour
½ teaspoon browning and
    seasoning sauce

Heat the oil in a 6-quart pressure cooker over high heat. Add the meat, sprinkle with the salt and pepper, and brown, uncovered, for 8 to 10 minutes. Remove the pressure cooker from the heat. Add the potatoes, carrots, onions, broth, and 1 cup water. Lock the lid in place and bring to full pressure over high heat. When the pressure regulator begins to rock, reduce the heat to medium and cook for 8 minutes. Remove from the heat and allow the pressure to drop slowly until steam no longer escapes from the vent and the pressure is completely reduced. In a small bowl, combine the remaining ½ cup water, the flour, and browning and seasoning sauce. Remove the lid from the pressure cooker and stir the flour mixture into the stew. Cook, stirring, over medium heat, uncovered, for 8 to 10 minutes, or until thickened.

Chunky Beef and Bean Chili

4 to 6 servings

Here's a chili that'll leave you feeling as if you've been out on the range with the cowboys. So go to it, Pardner!

¼ cup vegetable oil
5 pounds boneless beef chuck
    steak or roast, cut into
    1-inch cubes
4 large onions, coarsely
    chopped
4 garlic cloves, minced

2 bay leaves
5 tablespoons chili powder
1½ teaspoons ground cumin
1 teaspoon salt
¾ teaspoon cayenne pepper
3 cans (15 ounces each) red
    kidney beans, drained

Heat the oil in a 6-quart pressure cooker over high heat. Add the meat and brown, uncovered, for 8 to 10 minutes, stirring occasionally. Add the remaining ingredients except the kidney beans; mix well. Lock the lid in place and bring to full pressure over high heat. When the pressure regulator begins to rock, reduce the heat to medium and cook for 16 minutes. Remove from the heat and allow the pressure to drop slowly until steam no longer escapes from the vent and the pressure is completely reduced. Remove the lid and stir in the beans. Cook over medium-low heat, uncovered, for 4 to 5 minutes, or until the beans are heated through. **Be sure to discard the bay leaves before serving.**

NOTE: For real down-home chili, top this with some sour cream, chopped onions, or shredded cheese—or, better yet, all three!

Beefy-Good Onion Soup

4 to 6 servings

No tears from this onion dish! And the beefy flavor makes it soup-er delicious.

1 cup (2 sticks) butter
8 medium-sized onions, cut in half and thinly sliced
1½ teaspoons salt
½ teaspoon black pepper
1 pound boneless beef chuck steak, cut into ¾-inch chunks
4 cans (10½ ounces each) condensed beef broth

Melt the butter in a 6-quart pressure cooker and add the onions; sprinkle with the salt and pepper and sauté over high heat for 10 to 12 minutes, uncovered, or until the onions are golden. Remove to a bowl and set aside. Add the beef and brown, uncovered, for 5 minutes. Stir in the broth. Lock the lid in place and bring to full pressure over high heat. When the pressure regulator begins to rock, reduce the heat to medium and cook for 15 minutes. Cool the cooker at once by placing under cold running water until steam no longer escapes from the vent and the pressure is completely reduced. Remove the lid. Return the onions to the pot and heat over medium heat, uncovered, until the onions are warmed through.

NOTE: For an easy traditional cheese topping, place a slice of Swiss cheese on top of each of 4 to 6 slices of French bread and broil in a toaster oven until the cheese melts. Carefully place each piece of bread over a bowl of soup and serve immediately.

Braised Short Ribs

5 to 6 servings

If you love ribs like I do, you want to try all the best recipes . . . and this is one of 'em!

3 tablespoons vegetable oil
3½ pounds beef short ribs
¼ cup water
1¼ cups ketchup
⅓ cup prepared yellow
    mustard

½ cup firmly packed light
    brown sugar
2 cans (15 ounces each) whole
    potatoes, drained
1 package (10 ounces) frozen
    lima beans, thawed

Heat the oil in a 6-quart pressure cooker over high heat. Add the short ribs and cook, uncovered, for 8 to 10 minutes, or until browned on all sides. Add the water. Lock the lid in place and bring to full pressure over high heat. When the pressure regulator begins to rock, reduce the heat to medium and cook for 35 minutes. Cool the cooker at once by placing under cold running water until steam no longer escapes from the vent and the pressure is completely reduced. Remove the lid and drain off the excess liquid. In a medium-sized bowl, combine the ketchup, mustard, and brown sugar. Add to the ribs along with the potatoes and lima beans; mix well. Bring to a boil over high heat, uncovered, then reduce the heat to low and simmer for 6 to 8 minutes, or until the vegetables are heated through. Remove to a serving platter and serve immediately.

Heat-'em-Up Chili

4 to 6 servings

I know you've already got a favorite chili recipe, but most of them need to cook for hours and hours. So when you want to heat up your gang's taste buds in a hurry, this one'll be at the top of your list!

1 tablespoon vegetable oil
1½ pounds ground beef
1 large green bell pepper, coarsely chopped
1 large onion, coarsely chopped
1 can (14½ ounces) diced tomatoes, undrained

1 can (15 ounces) tomato sauce
3 tablespoons chili powder
2 teaspoons ground cumin
½ teaspoon salt
½ teaspoon black pepper
1 can (15 ounces) red kidney beans, drained

Heat the oil in a 6-quart pressure cooker over high heat. Brown the beef, uncovered, for 8 to 10 minutes; drain off the excess liquid. Add the remaining ingredients except the kidney beans; mix well. Lock the lid in place and bring to full pressure over high heat. When the pressure regulator begins to rock, reduce the heat to medium and cook for 5 minutes. Cool the cooker at once by placing under cold running water until steam no longer escapes from the vent and the pressure is completely reduced. Remove the lid and stir in the kidney beans; allow to sit for 5 minutes, then serve immediately.

St. Patrick's Day Special

4 to 6 servings

Heard of the blue plate special? Well, I especially love this St. Patrick's Day special. And I have it every year in Chicago 'cause I spend every St. Patrick's Day there, marching in the parade and enjoying the great food and festivities!

One 3-pound uncooked corned beef with pickling spices and juice
2½ cups water, divided
1 large head cabbage, quartered
4 large carrots, cut into 3-inch chunks
6 medium-sized potatoes, peeled and cut in half
½ teaspoon salt
¼ teaspoon black pepper

Place the corned beef with the pickling spices and 2 cups water in a 6-quart pressure cooker. Lock the lid in place and bring to full pressure over high heat. When the pressure regulator begins to rock, reduce the heat to medium and cook for 60 minutes. Cool the cooker at once by placing under cold running water until steam no longer escapes from the vent and the pressure is completely reduced. Remove the lid; place the corned beef on a serving platter and cover to keep warm. Add the remaining ½ cup water and the remaining ingredients to the pressure cooker. Lock the lid in place and bring to full pressure over high heat. When the pressure regulator begins to rock, reduce the heat to medium and cook for 4 minutes. Cool the cooker at once, as above. Remove the lid; with a slotted spoon, remove the vegetables to the serving platter. Slice the corned beef against the grain and serve with the vegetables.

Eggplant and Veal with Penne

If you shy away from making eggplant because you know only one way to prepare it, it's time to team it with some new friends. You'll have a real hit on your hands . . . promise!

3 tablespoons olive oil
2 medium-sized onions, coarsely chopped
2 pounds veal stew meat, trimmed and cut into 1-inch chunks
1 medium-sized eggplant, peeled and cut into 1-inch chunks

1 can (4¼ ounces) chopped black olives, drained
1 jar (26 ounces) spaghetti sauce
3 tablespoons lemon juice
½ teaspoon salt
1 pound penne pasta, cooked, drained, and kept warm

Heat the oil in a 6-quart pressure cooker over high heat. Add the onions and veal and cook, uncovered, stirring occasionally, for 10 to 12 minutes, or until the veal is no longer pink. Add the remaining ingredients except the pasta. Lock the lid in place and bring to full pressure over high heat. When the pressure regulator begins to rock, reduce the heat to medium and cook for 8 minutes. Cool the cooker at once by placing under cold running water until steam no longer escapes from the vent and the pressure is completely reduced. Remove the lid, stir in the pasta, and serve.

Greek Lamb

4 to 5 servings

When I think of Greece, I think of beautiful seashores, friendly people, and, oh yes—fabulous food! And this dish sure tastes like the real thing!

1 tablespoon olive oil
2 pounds lamb stew meat, trimmed and cut into 1-inch chunks
1 large onion, cut into wedges
2 garlic cloves, minced
4 medium-sized red potatoes, quartered
4 medium-sized carrots, cut into ½-inch chunks

½ cup dry red wine
¼ teaspoon browning and seasoning sauce
1 teaspoon ground cumin
½ teaspoon black pepper
1 cup sliced green olives with pimientos, drained

Heat the oil in a 6-quart pressure cooker over high heat. Add the lamb, onion, and garlic and sauté, uncovered, for 10 to 12 minutes, or until the lamb is lightly browned on all sides. Add the remaining ingredients except the olives; mix well. Lock the lid in place and bring to full pressure over high heat. When the pressure regulator begins to rock, reduce the heat to medium and cook for 10 minutes. Cool the cooker at once by placing under cold running water until steam no longer escapes from the vent and the pressure is completely reduced. Remove the lid and stir in the olives. Cook, uncovered, over medium-high heat for 5 to 6 minutes to reduce and thicken the juices; serve immediately.

NOTE: For added Greek flavor, sprinkle with some crumbled feta cheese just before serving.

Pork Roast Dinner

4 to 6 servings

Boy oh boy! There's no mystery as to why they're gonna love these tender pork tidbits. After all, they soak up the most incredible flavors while cooking. What a soothing blend of lip-smackin' good eating!

One 4-pound center-cut pork roast, ribs cracked (see Note)
1 teaspoon salt
1½ teaspoons black pepper, divided
2 tablespoons vegetable oil
1 medium-sized onion, cut into ¼-inch slices
2 cups water
2 medium-sized yellow squash, cut into 1½-inch chunks
1 medium-sized zucchini, cut into 1½-inch chunks
2 cans (15 ounces each) whole potatoes, drained
1 teaspoon onion powder

Sprinkle the pork with the salt and 1 ßteaspoon pepper. Heat the oil in a 6-quart pressure cooker over medium-high heat. Brown the pork roast, uncovered, for 8 to 10 minutes. Place the onion slices over the roast and add the water. Lock the lid in place and bring to full pressure over high heat. When the pressure regulator begins to rock, reduce the heat to medium and cook for 45 to 50 minutes. Cool the cooker at once by placing under cold running water until steam no longer escapes from the vent and the pressure is completely reduced. Remove the lid and place the roast on a serving platter; cover to keep warm. Add the remaining ingredients, including the remaining ½ teaspoon pepper, to the pressure cooker. Cook, uncovered, for 8 to 10 minutes over medium-high heat, or until the vegetables are fork-tender. Slice the roast and serve with the vegetables and cooking liquid.

NOTE: Make sure to ask the butcher to crack the ribs on the pork roast for you—it makes cutting the roast much easier. Or, if you prefer, use a boneless pork roast.

Apple-Sauerkraut Pork Chops

4 servings

What a combination! The sweetness of the apples sets off the tartness of the sauerkraut just right.

2 tablespoons vegetable oil
4 pork loin chops (1¼ to 1½ pounds total), ¾ inch thick
½ teaspoon salt
¼ teaspoon black pepper
3 medium-sized sweet potatoes (about 1½ pounds), peeled and cut into 2-inch chunks
3 Red Delicious apples, peeled, cored, and cut in half
½ cup apple juice
½ cup firmly packed light brown sugar
2 teaspoons ground cinnamon
About 2 pounds sauerkraut, rinsed, drained, and squeezed dry

Heat the oil in a 6-quart pressure cooker over high heat. Sprinkle the pork chops with the salt and pepper. Add 2 of the chops to the pressure cooker and brown, uncovered, for 4 to 6 minutes, turning halfway through the cooking. Remove to a platter and brown the remaining chops. Place the sweet potatoes in the bottom of the pressure cooker, then layer the pork chops and apples on top. In a small bowl, combine the apple juice, brown sugar, and cinnamon; mix well and pour over the pork chops. Top with the sauerkraut, making sure not to fill the cooker more than two-thirds full. Lock the lid in place and bring to full pressure over high heat. When the pressure regulator begins to rock, reduce the heat to medium and cook for 10 minutes. Cool the cooker at once by placing under cold running water until steam no longer escapes from the vent and the pressure is completely reduced. Remove the lid and serve the pork chops with the sweet potatoes, apples, and sauerkraut, spooning the sauce over the top.

Flavor-Packed Brunswick Stew

4 to 6 servings

Unlock the lid and unlock all the goodness of this chicken and vegetable stew. Your family's cleaned plates and smiling faces will be quite a reward!

1 can (14½ ounces) ready-to-use chicken broth

1 can (14½ ounces) whole tomatoes, chopped, juice reserved

1 chicken (3 to 3½ pounds), cut into 8 pieces and skin removed

5 medium-sized carrots, cut into ½-inch chunks

1 large onion, finely chopped

1 package (16 ounces) frozen lima beans, thawed

3 bay leaves

½ teaspoon ground thyme

1½ teaspoons salt

¼ teaspoon cayenne pepper

3 medium-sized sweet potatoes (about 1½ pounds), peeled and cut into 2-inch chunks

2 packages (10 ounces each) frozen cream-style corn, thawed

½ cup chopped fresh parsley

In a 6-quart pressure cooker, combine the broth, tomatoes and their juice, the chicken, carrots, onion, lima beans, bay leaves, thyme, salt, and cayenne pepper; mix well. Place the sweet potatoes on top. Lock the lid in place and bring to full pressure over high heat. When the pressure regulator begins to rock, reduce the heat to medium and cook for 8 minutes. Cool the cooker at once by placing under cold running water until steam no longer escapes from the vent and the pressure is completely reduced. Remove the lid. Stir in the corn and parsley and cook, uncovered, over medium-high heat for 8 to 10 minutes, or until the corn is warmed through. **Be sure to discard the bay leaves before serving.**

Stuffed Cornish Hens

2 to 4 servings

You want simple and elegant? This is the meal for you!

2 cups five-minute stuffing
   mix
1 cup hot water
2 Cornish hens (about
   1½ pounds each)
1 teaspoon salt

1 teaspoon black pepper
2 tablespoons vegetable oil
½ cup water
4 medium-sized carrots, cut
   into 2-inch pieces
1 teaspoon onion powder

In a medium-sized bowl, combine the stuffing mix with the water until moistened. Place half of the stuffing mixture in each Cornish hen. Rub the salt and pepper evenly over the hens. Heat the oil in a 6-quart pressure cooker over medium-high heat and brown the hens, uncovered, for 8 to 10 minutes, turning several times, to brown on all sides. Remove the hens from the pressure cooker and add the water and carrots. Return the hens to the cooker and sprinkle with the onion powder. Lock the lid in place and bring to full pressure over high heat. When the pressure regulator begins to rock, reduce the heat to medium and cook for 7 minutes. Remove from the heat and allow the pressure to drop slowly until steam no longer escapes from the vent and the pressure is completely reduced. Remove the lid and serve each hen whole or cut in half.

NOTE: If the Cornish hens are frozen, make sure to thaw completely before stuffing.

Lemon-Steamed Swordfish

4 to 6 servings

There's nothing fishy about this one, except that you're gonna reel them in hook, line, and sinker with the hint of fresh lemon.

1 cup dry white wine
¼ cup lemon juice
¼ cup water
4 swordfish steaks (about 2
    pounds total), ¾ inch thick
1 teaspoon dried dillweed

1½ teaspoons salt, divided
½ teaspoon black pepper
1 bunch broccoli, cut into
    large florets
4 medium-sized red potatoes,
    quartered

Place the steaming rack in a 6-quart pressure cooker and add the wine, lemon juice, and water. Place the swordfish on the rack and sprinkle with the dillweed, ½ teaspoon salt, and the pepper. Place the broccoli and potatoes over the fish and sprinkle with the remaining 1 teaspoon salt. Lock the lid in place and bring to full pressure over high heat. When the pressure regulator begins to rock, reduce the heat to medium and cook for 1½ minutes. Cool the cooker at once by placing under cold running water until steam no longer escapes from the vent and the pressure is completely reduced. Remove the lid. Carefully remove the fish and vegetables to a serving platter. Serve immediately.

NOTE: For an extra touch of flavor, cut a lemon in half and squeeze over the finished dish just before serving.

The Wok

Stirring It Up

So many people hear about cooking in a wok and have no idea how to do it. Basically, a wok is a shallow, bowl-shaped pan that is used to quick-cook food. There are portable electric woks that work by themselves, without taking up cooking space on the stovetop, but traditional woks are used over a gas or electric stove element.

Because you can cook food in a wok at a very high temperature, the surface area of the pan gets extremely hot and cooks food very quickly. In this chapter I've got quite a few traditional wok favorites, but I've also got untraditional ones, like Veal Orzo Stir-fry (page 86). So, whether you're heading out to buy a wok or rediscovering an old kitchen friend, check out my tips below:

- A heavy wok will distribute heat more evenly than a thin one, avoiding hot spots and uneven cooking.

- Make sure the wok sits securely on its ring over the heat source; you don't want it to rock!

- Since woks cook food so fast, be sure to have all ingredients prepared, cut, and ready before starting to cook. Make sure that the food to be cooked is all cut to approximately the same size so it'll cook evenly.

- Always preheat the oil in the wok and, if adding additional oil while cooking, pour it around the top inside edge of the wok, allowing it to trickle down over the cooking surface.

- Woks can be used as deep skillets, too, so they're very handy. Keep yours available in your kitchen.

- After each use, it's best to wash or simply rinse, not scrub, the inside of a wok. Dry immediately. When it's dry, rub the inside with a thin coating of vegetable oil before storing.

The Wok

Stirring It Up

Teriyaki Steak

When I want to make sure that everyone gets plenty of veggies, I serve up these sizzling steak strips in tangy Asian-flavored sauce. You should, too!

½ cup plus 2 tablespoons soy sauce, divided
¼ cup vegetable oil, divided
¼ cup dry sherry or dry white wine
2 tablespoons molasses
2 garlic cloves, crushed
½ teaspoon ground ginger

1½ pounds beef flank steak, cut lengthwise in half, then crosswise into ¼-inch strips
½ cup all-purpose flour
1 teaspoon black pepper
2 packages (16 ounces each) frozen stir-fry vegetables, thawed
½ cup water

In a large bowl, combine ½ cup soy sauce, 2 tablespoons oil, the sherry, molasses, garlic, and ginger; mix well. Add the beef strips and toss to coat. Cover and marinate in the refrigerator for at least 2 hours, or overnight. In a large resealable plastic storage bag, combine the flour and pepper; mix well. Drain the beef strips, discarding the marinade, and place in the bag with the flour mixture. Seal and toss to coat completely. Heat the remaining 2 tablespoons oil just until hot in a wok over medium-high heat or in an electric wok that has been preheated to 400°F. Brown the beef for 4 to 6 minutes, stirring occasionally. Add the vegetables and cook for 4 to 6 minutes, or until the vegetables are crisp-tender. Stir in the water and the remaining 2 tablespoons soy sauce until thickened.

NOTE: Serve over chow mein noodles or hot cooked rice.

Beefed-Up Tropical Fried Rice

4 to 6 servings

When the tastes of Asia blend with the tastes of the tropics, we get a very special meal.

2 tablespoons vegetable oil
1 pound beef flank steak, cut
   lengthwise in half, then
   crosswise into thin strips
2 garlic cloves, minced
1 teaspoon crushed red pepper
½ teaspoon ground ginger
1 package (16 ounces) frozen
   peas and carrots, thawed

3 cups cold cooked rice
½ cup soy sauce
3 tablespoons sugar
1 can (8 ounces) pineapple
   tidbits in juice, drained
   and juice reserved (see
   Note)

Heat the oil just until hot in a wok over medium-high heat or in an electric wok that has been preheated to 400°F. Add the beef, garlic, red pepper, and ginger and sauté for 4 to 5 minutes, or until the beef is browned. Stir in the peas and carrots, rice, and soy sauce until thoroughly mixed. In a small bowl, combine the sugar and the reserved pineapple juice, then add to the wok with the pineapple tidbits, stirring until combined. Cook for 4 to 5 minutes, or until thoroughly heated.

NOTE: Can't find pineapple tidbits in the market? Just cut chunks or rings into small pieces. And if you'd like to add a little more color, sprinkle this with thinly sliced scallions just before serving.

Veal Orzo Stir-fry

4 to 6 servings

If you think only Chinese food is made in a wok, keep your chopsticks handy for this Italian goodie. What a stir-fry surprise . . . tender morsels of veal tossed with tiny pasta in a scrumptious sauce.

4 cups water
1 pound orzo pasta
¼ cup vegetable oil
2 medium-sized onions, cut into wedges
2 medium-sized bell peppers (1 red and 1 green), cut into ½-inch strips
½ pound fresh mushrooms, cut into quarters

1 pound veal cutlets, slightly pounded and cut across the grain into ¼-inch strips
½ teaspoon garlic powder
½ teaspoon salt
½ teaspoon black pepper
1 jar (26 ounces) spaghetti sauce

Preheat a wok over medium-high heat or preheat an electric wok to 400°F. Add the water and bring to a boil. Add the orzo, cover, and cook for 8 to 10 minutes, or until tender. Drain the orzo and set aside on a platter; cover to keep warm. Heat the oil in the wok and add the onions, bell peppers, and mushrooms; stir-fry for 8 to 10 minutes, or until tender. Stir in the veal, garlic powder, salt, and black pepper and cook for 6 to 8 minutes, or until the veal is cooked through. Stir in the spaghetti sauce and heat for 4 to 5 minutes, until the sauce is hot. Serve over the orzo.

NOTE: Make sure to buy thin veal cutlets or to pound them until they are thin.

Sweet-and-Sour Pork

4 to 6 servings

Now you can make this restaurant favorite at home anytime you want it!

2 tablespoons vegetable oil
1½ pounds boneless pork loin,
    cut into ½" × 3" strips
2 tablespoons ketchup
¼ cup honey
1 can (20 ounces) pineapple
    chunks in juice, undrained

2 large red bell peppers, cut
    into thin strips
3 tablespoons soy sauce
1 tablespoon cornstarch

Preheat a wok over medium-high heat or preheat an electric wok to 400°F. Heat the oil until hot but not smoking. Add the pork and cook for 4 to 5 minutes, until browned, stirring occasionally. Add the ketchup, honey, pineapple and its juice, and the red peppers; cook for 5 to 7 minutes, or until the sauce comes to a boil. In a small bowl, combine the soy sauce and cornstarch; whisk well. Add the cornstarch mixture to the wok; mix well. Cook for 2 to 3 minutes, or until the sauce thickens.

NOTE: I like to top this with scallions cut into 1-inch pieces.

Chinatown Pork and Fried Rice

3 to 4 servings

A wise man once said, "You'll save time and money when you make it yourself." Okay, let's be wise! This is just like the restaurant version, but without the bill at the end of the meal!

3 tablespoons vegetable oil
1½ cups uncooked long- or whole-grain rice
1 medium-sized onion, chopped
2 celery stalks, chopped
1 pork tenderloin (¾ to 1 pound), cut into ¼-inch slices

2 cups hot water
1 beef bouillon cube
¼ cup soy sauce
1 medium-sized green bell pepper, cut into 1-inch chunks
½ pound fresh mushrooms, sliced

Heat the oil just until hot in a wok over medium-high heat or in an electric wok that has been preheated to 400°F. Stir in the rice, onion, and celery and cook, stirring occasionally, for about 10 minutes, or until the rice is golden. Add the pork and cook for 5 minutes, or until browned, stirring occasionally. Add the hot water, bouillon cube, and soy sauce; mix well. Bring to a boil, reduce the heat to low, cover, and simmer for about 20 minutes, or until the water is absorbed. Add the pepper and mushrooms; stir until well mixed. Cover and cook for 8 to 10 minutes, or until the vegetables are crisp-tender. Serve immediately.

NOTE: Make sure to use pork tenderloin, not pork loin.

Tempura Chicken and Vegetables

4 to 6 servings

Tempura is great because it works with almost any type of vegetable (although firm ones work best). If your favorite isn't included, just substitute it for one of the ones used here.

5 cups biscuit baking mix
1½ teaspoons cayenne pepper
1 teaspoon garlic powder
2 teaspoons salt
2½ cups (20 ounces) club soda
1½ pounds boneless, skinless chicken breasts, cut into ½-inch strips
1 bunch broccoli, cut into florets
½ pound whole fresh mushrooms
1 medium-sized zucchini, cut into ½" × 3" sticks
1 can (15 ounces) whole potatoes, drained and cut in half
3 cups vegetable oil for deep-frying

In a large bowl, combine the baking mix, cayenne pepper, garlic powder, and salt. Add the club soda; mix well. Add the remaining ingredients except the oil; stir to coat completely. Heat the oil just until hot in a wok over medium-high heat or in an electric wok that has been preheated to 400°F. Let the excess batter drip off the chicken and vegetables before placing them in the hot oil one piece at a time until the wok is barely full; do not overcrowd the wok. Cook for 8 to 10 minutes, or until the coating is golden brown and the chicken is cooked through. Remove with a slotted spoon and drain on paper towels. Continue with the remaining chicken and vegetables until all are cooked; discard any remaining batter. Serve immediately, or keep warm on a baking sheet in a 150°F. oven for up to 1 hour before serving.

Crunchy Cashew Chicken

4 servings

Want to see some eyes light up? Let 'em take a bite out of this light and crunchy Asian chicken favorite. Served over warm rice and sprinkled with chow mein noodles, it makes a great quick meal.

1 egg
2 tablespoons soy sauce
1 tablespoon cornstarch
1½ pounds boneless, skinless chicken breasts, cut into ½-inch chunks
¼ cup peanut oil
½ pound fresh mushrooms, quartered

1 large green bell pepper, diced
1 can (8 ounces) water chestnuts, drained
½ cup roasted cashews
2 tablespoons hoisin sauce

In a large bowl, combine the egg, soy sauce, and cornstarch. Whisk well, then add the chicken and toss to coat. Preheat a wok over medium-high heat or preheat an electric wok to 400°F. Heat the oil until hot, then add the chicken and soy sauce mixture. Cook, stirring constantly, for 4 to 5 minutes, or until no pink remains in the chicken. Add the remaining ingredients and cook for about 3 minutes, stirring until well mixed and warmed through.

Sweet-and-Sour Chicken

4 to 6 servings

You'll never "sour" on this "sweet"-heart of a recipe!

¼ cup all-purpose flour
½ teaspoon salt
¼ teaspoon black pepper
1½ pounds boneless, skinless
    chicken breasts, cut into
    ½-inch strips
3 tablespoons vegetable oil
1 package (16 ounces) frozen
    stir-fry vegetables, thawed
    (see Note)

1½ cups sweet-and-sour (duck)
    sauce
1½ teaspoons soy sauce
1 teaspoon ground ginger
1½ cups water
2 packages (3 ounces each)
    ramen noodles, broken
    into pieces

In a shallow bowl, combine the flour, salt, and pepper; mix well. Coat the chicken evenly on all sides with the flour mixture. Heat the oil just until hot in a wok over medium-high heat or in an electric wok that has been preheated to 400°F. Stir-fry the coated chicken for 10 to 12 minutes, or until golden. Stir in the vegetables, sweet-and-sour sauce, soy sauce, and ginger; mix well. Add the water and noodles (reserve the noodle seasoning packets for another use); stir until well coated. Cover and reduce the heat to low. Simmer for 8 to 10 minutes, or until the noodles are tender.

NOTE: Use the frozen vegetable mix that includes your favorites—either broccoli, carrots, and water chestnuts or snow peas, carrots, and bell peppers.

Shrimp Special Fried Rice

4 to 5 servings

I love stir-frying because it brings quick excitement to foods as plain as rice! It'll make you feel like a professional chef. Wanna know the secret to making it look as good as it tastes? The shrimp and eggs. Sshh!

½ cup peanut oil
8 cups cold cooked rice
8 scallions, thinly sliced
½ cup soy sauce
½ teaspoon sugar

4 eggs, beaten
1 package (10 ounces) frozen
    cooked shrimp, thawed
    and drained

Heat the oil just until hot in a wok over medium-high heat or in an electric wok that has been preheated to 400°F. Add the rice, scallions, soy sauce, and sugar and cook for 5 to 6 minutes, or until very hot, stirring constantly. Slowly add the eggs, stirring constantly, and cook, stirring, for 3 to 4 minutes, or until the eggs are cooked and the ingredients are well combined. Add the shrimp and cook for 1 to 2 minutes, or until heated through.

NOTE: For the best fried rice, cook your rice ahead of time and make sure it is well chilled before stir-frying.

Vegetable Stir-fry

4 to 6 servings

All the fresh veggies in this recipe will get your appetite going . . . right back to the wok for seconds!

1 can (15 ounces) baby corn, drained and liquid reserved
1 tablespoon sesame oil
2 tablespoons soy sauce
1 tablespoon sugar
2 tablespoons cornstarch
⅓ cup peanut oil
1 garlic clove, minced

1 bunch broccoli, cut into small florets
½ pound fresh mushrooms, cut into ¼-inch slices
2 medium-sized bell peppers (1 red and 1 yellow), cut into ½-inch strips
1 large onion, cut into wedges
½ pound snow peas, trimmed

In a small bowl, combine the reserved liquid from the corn, the sesame oil, soy sauce, sugar, and cornstarch; mix well and set aside. Heat the oil just until hot in a wok over medium-high heat or in an electric wok that has been pre-heated to 400°F. Add the garlic, broccoli, mushrooms, peppers, and onion. Cook, stirring constantly, for 5 to 6 minutes, or until the vegetables are crisp-tender. Add the snow peas and baby corn and continue cooking and stirring for 3 to 4 minutes, or until the snow peas turn bright green. Add the soy sauce mixture, then stir and cook for 2 to 3 minutes, or until the sauce thickens. Serve immediately.

The Pasta Pot

Using Your Noodles

Who doesn't like pasta? I mean, most of us grew up eating *some* type of pasta. It's versatile enough to be used in countless great side dishes, yet as a main course, pasta's a real treat, too. And since each of the pasta recipes that follows is made in just one pot, that means that the pasta and, yes, all the other ingredients, all go into one pot. Wow! Is that ever a big help when it comes to cleanup!

Now don't think of pasta as just spaghetti, 'cause I've got pasta recipes here that use twists, elbows, wiggles . . . and some dishes are so fancy that they call for bow ties! But whatever pasta is your passion, here are a few pointers for when the recipe says to start out by making the pasta "according to the package directions":

- Generally, cook pasta in a large pot of boiling salted water, allowing about 1 quart of water for every ¼ pound of pasta.

- Slip the pasta into the boiling water a little at a time so that the water keeps boiling.

- Stir immediately so the pasta won't stick together; then stir occasionally, checking for doneness.

To check pasta for doneness:

- Cook it until still firm if it's going into a dish where it will continue to cook. You won't want to overcook it, since then it'll absorb the maximum amount of cooking water and your finished dish can become watery.

- Test pasta by cutting a piece with a fork, or taking a bite. When it has only a slight bit of uncooked core, it is considered *al dente*, as Italians say, or "to the tooth." (It means there's something to chew.)

Oh, I almost forgot—since all the ingredients in these recipes are cooked in one pot, these dishes are best when served immediately. If letting the dish stand for any length of time, you may want to add a bit more sauce or liquid to the recipe.

The Pasta Pot

Using Your Noodles

No-Wait Spaghetti with Meat Sauce

6 to 8 servings

I don't know anyone who doesn't love spaghetti. And now we don't have to feel as if we're missing out on homemade flavor when we rush to open a jar of sauce. It helps to keep this one convenient, 'cause we use it to make a zesty meat sauce that cooks up in the same pot as the pasta!

1 pound spaghetti
2 tablespoons olive oil
1 pound ground beef
1 large green bell pepper, chopped
1 large onion, chopped
1 medium-sized carrot, shredded
1 jar (26 ounces) spaghetti sauce
1 teaspoon garlic powder

In a 6-quart soup pot, cook the pasta according to the package directions; drain, rinse, drain again, and set aside in the colander. In the same pot, heat the oil over high heat and cook the ground beef, pepper, onion, and carrot for 8 to 10 minutes, or until no pink remains in the beef. Add the spaghetti sauce and garlic powder and reduce the heat to medium-low, stirring to combine thoroughly. Return the pasta to the pot and toss to coat; cook for 2 to 3 minutes, or until the pasta is warmed through.

Mexican Beef and Noodles

4 to 6 servings

It's kind of like a Mexican stroganoff, and a lot easier than the Hungarian version . . . lighter, too!

1 pound medium egg noodles
1½ pounds ground beef
1 jar (12 ounces) salsa
1 jar (26 ounces) spaghetti
    sauce with mushrooms

1 can (3.8 ounces) sliced black
    olives, drained
1 cup (4 ounces) shredded
    Cheddar cheese

In a 6-quart soup pot, cook the noodles according to the package directions; drain, rinse, drain again, and set aside in the colander. In the same pot, brown the beef over high heat for 5 to 7 minutes, or until no pink remains. Stir in the salsa, spaghetti sauce, and olives, then return the noodles to the pot. Reduce the heat to medium and cook for 3 to 5 minutes, stirring, until thoroughly combined and heated through. Top with the cheese and serve.

NOTE: This is the perfect dish to make ahead and freeze. Just transfer it to a foil pan, cover well, and freeze until needed.

Wintry Beef 'n' Bean Pasta

4 to 6 servings

When it's cold outside and you want to serve up some stick-to-your-ribs goodness, throw together this comforting combination of meat, beans, and pasta. With a bowl of this and some warm, crusty bread, you'll be all set to curl up by the fire.

¼ cup vegetable oil
1 pound ground beef
4 garlic cloves, coarsely chopped
1 can (14½ ounces) diced tomatoes, undrained
1 can (14½ ounces) ready-to-use chicken broth
1 cup water
½ teaspoon browning and seasoning sauce

2 cans (14 to 16 ounces each) cannellini beans (white kidney beans), undrained
½ cup chopped fresh parsley
4 teaspoons dried oregano
1½ teaspoons black pepper
8 ounces elbow pasta
½ cup grated Parmesan cheese

In a 6-quart soup pot, heat the oil over medium-high heat. Add the ground beef and garlic and brown for 4 to 6 minutes, or until no pink remains in the beef. Add the tomatoes, broth, water, browning and seasoning sauce, beans, parsley, oregano, and pepper; mix well. Bring to a boil and add the pasta. Cook for 10 to 12 minutes, or until the pasta is tender. Stir in the Parmesan cheese and serve in bowls.

Lamb Couscous

4 to 6 servings

This dish will have you dreaming about exotic Moroccan adventures. (No travel agents needed for this trip, either!)

2 to 2½ pounds lamb stew meat or boneless leg of lamb, cut into 1-inch chunks

1 medium-sized onion, coarsely chopped

3 garlic cloves, minced

1 can (28 ounces) crushed tomatoes

1 can (14½ ounces) ready-to-use beef broth

1 package (16 ounces) frozen mixed vegetables

1 teaspoon ground cinnamon

1 teaspoon salt

½ teaspoon black pepper

1 package (10 ounces) couscous (see Note)

Spray a 6-quart soup pot with nonstick vegetable spray, then brown the lamb, onion, and garlic for 8 to 10 minutes over medium-high heat, or until no pink remains in the lamb. Add the remaining ingredients except the couscous and bring to a boil. Reduce the heat to low, cover, and simmer for 55 to 60 minutes, or until the lamb is fork-tender. Stir in the couscous and simmer for 4 to 5 minutes, or until the couscous is tender.

NOTE: Couscous is a Moroccan pasta that can usually be found next to the rice and regular pasta in your grocery store.

Spicy Rigatoni

4 to 6 servings

When you want to set the world on fire—or maybe just your taste buds—hot Italian sausage can do the trick! Pasta with just the right fixin's makes this a dish that looks as good as it tastes.

1 pound rigatoni pasta
1 tablespoon vegetable oil
1 pound hot Italian pork
    sausage, casings removed
    (see Note)
1 bunch broccoli, cut into
    florets
1 large onion, thinly sliced

1 can (14½ ounces) ready-to-
    use chicken broth
½ teaspoon garlic powder
1 teaspoon salt
3 cans (15 ounces each)
    Great Northern beans,
    undrained

In a 6-quart soup pot, cook the pasta according to the package directions; drain, rinse, drain again, and set aside in the colander. In the same pot, heat the oil over medium-high heat and add the sausage, broccoli, and onion. Sauté for 12 to 15 minutes, or until the sausage is no longer pink and the vegetables are tender. Reduce the heat to medium and add the broth, garlic powder, and salt; mix well. Add the beans and return the pasta to the pot, stirring until thoroughly mixed. Simmer for 8 to 10 minutes, or until the sauce thickens and the pasta and beans are warmed through.

NOTE: I like to use pork sausage in this recipe, but any kind of spicy Italian sausage will work well. Or keep the fat content down by substituting turkey sausage for pork.

Spinach Fettuccine Carbonara

3 to 4 servings

So few ingredients . . . such simple directions . . . such fabulous taste!

½ pound bacon
12 ounces spinach fettuccine
½ cup (1 stick) butter
2 cups (1 pint) heavy cream
1½ cups grated Parmesan
    cheese

½ teaspoon black pepper
1 package (10 ounces) frozen
    peas, thawed and drained

In a 6-quart soup pot, cook the bacon over medium heat for 3 to 5 minutes, or until brown and crisp; remove to paper towels to drain. Drain off the fat from the pot. In the same pot, cook the fettuccine according to the package directions; drain, rinse, drain again, and set aside in the colander. In the same pot, melt the butter over low heat. Stir in the cream, Parmesan cheese, and pepper. Cook for 2 to 3 minutes, or until hot and slightly thickened, stirring frequently. Return the pasta to the pot and add the peas, stirring until thoroughly mixed and warmed through. Crumble the bacon over the pasta, toss, and serve immediately.

NOTE: Leave the bacon and peas out and you'll have a quick and easy Fettuccine Alfredo.

Gorgonzola Twist

4 to 6 servings

You've heard of the dances the "Swim" and the "Mashed Potato"? Well, it's time to do the "Gorgonzola Twist." It's perky pasta twists mixed with creamy Gorgonzola cheese. Sure, one taste will be enough to make you feel like dancing!

12 ounces pasta twists (rotini)
2 tablespoons olive oil
1 pound turkey cutlets, cut
    into ¼-inch strips
1 teaspoon minced garlic
1 pound fresh mushrooms,
    quartered
3 cups broccoli florets
½ cup oil-packed sun-dried
    tomatoes, drained and
    thinly sliced
1 teaspoon salt
1 teaspoon black pepper
2 cups (10 ounces) crumbled
    Gorgonzola or blue cheese
1½ cups sour cream

In a 6-quart soup pot, cook the pasta according to the package directions; drain, rinse, drain again, and set aside in the colander. In the same pot, heat the oil over medium-high heat and sauté the turkey and garlic for 3 to 4 minutes, or until the turkey is no longer pink, stirring occasionally. Add the mushrooms, broccoli, sun-dried tomatoes, salt, and pepper; mix well and cook for 6 to 8 minutes, or until the mushrooms and broccoli are tender. Stir in the cheese and sour cream; reduce the heat to low and stir until smooth and creamy. Return the pasta to the pot and stir until well coated and warmed through. Serve immediately.

Chicken and Pasta Primavera

4 to 6 servings

When you see how simple this is to make, you're gonna be singing Italian love songs. Go ahead—nobody can hear!

1 pound rigatoni pasta
1 tablespoon vegetable oil
1½ pounds boneless, skinless chicken breasts, cut into ¼-inch strips
2 cans (10¾ ounces each) condensed cream of chicken soup
1 cup milk
1 teaspoon dried basil
1 teaspoon garlic powder
½ teaspoon salt
½ teaspoon black pepper
1 package (16 ounces) frozen broccoli, cauliflower, and carrot combination, thawed
¼ cup grated Parmesan cheese

In a 6-quart soup pot, cook the pasta according to the package directions; drain, rinse, drain again, and set aside in the colander. In the same pot, heat the oil over medium-high heat and brown the chicken for 4 to 5 minutes. Add the remaining ingredients except the Parmesan cheese and pasta; mix well. Cook for 6 to 7 minutes, or until thoroughly heated, stirring occasionally. Return the pasta to the pot and cook for 4 to 5 minutes, or until heated through. Sprinkle with the Parmesan cheese and serve.

NOTE: Use your choice of frozen or fresh-cooked vegetables.

Pesto Chicken Pasta

4 to 6 servings

Pesto sauce has been on restaurant menus for quite a while, and now it's showing up on supermarket shelves everywhere. There's no need to wonder what to do with it, 'cause its nutty flavor complements so many dishes you won't know how you managed without it!

1 pound linguine
1 tablespoon vegetable oil
1½ pounds boneless, skinless
   chicken breasts, cut into
   1-inch chunks
2 teaspoons salt, divided

½ teaspoon black pepper
1 container (7 ounces) pesto
   sauce
1 cup (½ pint) heavy cream
7 plum tomatoes, cut into
   ¼-inch slices

In a 6-quart soup pot, cook the pasta according to the package directions; drain, rinse, drain again, and set aside in the colander. In the same pot, heat the oil over high heat and add the chicken; sprinkle it with 1 teaspoon salt and the pepper. Cook for 8 to 10 minutes, or until no pink remains in the chicken. Reduce the heat to medium-low and stir in the pesto, cream, and the remaining 1 teaspoon salt. Simmer for 2 to 3 minutes, then add the tomatoes and return the pasta to the pot, stirring until thoroughly combined. Cook for 3 to 5 minutes, or until the pasta is warmed through. Serve immediately.

Thai Chicken Pasta

4 to 6 servings

Yes, this sounds like an odd combination of ingredients, but once you taste the finished dish, you'll know it works!

1 pound linguine
⅓ cup plus 2 tablespoons
    sesame oil, divided
1½ pounds boneless, skinless
    chicken breasts, cut into
    1-inch cubes
1 cup crunchy peanut butter
⅔ cup heavy cream
¼ cup soy sauce
2 garlic cloves, minced

2 tablespoons white vinegar
1 tablespoon sugar
1 tablespoon ground ginger
1 tablespoon crushed red
    pepper
1 package (16 ounces) frozen
    broccoli, cauliflower, and
    carrot combination,
    thawed

In a 6-quart soup pot, cook the pasta according to the package directions; drain, rinse, drain again, and set aside in the colander. In the same pot, heat 2 tablespoons sesame oil over medium-high heat. Add the chicken and brown for 5 to 7 minutes. Meanwhile, in a medium-sized bowl, combine the peanut butter, cream, soy sauce, garlic, vinegar, the remaining ⅓ cup oil, the sugar, ginger, and red pepper; mix well. Add the vegetables to the chicken and cook for 4 to 5 minutes, or until the vegetables are tender. Return the linguine to the pot and add the peanut butter mixture; toss to coat. Reduce the heat to low and cook for 3 to 5 minutes, or until the mixture is thoroughly heated; do not boil.

NOTE: I like to top this with thinly sliced scallions for extra flavor and color.

Chicken Bott Boi

6 to 8 servings

Yes, Bott Boi is the real name for this traditional Pennsylvania Dutch dish. Because it's actually dressed-up bow-tie pasta and chunky veggies, I call it a great meal, too!

10 cups water
1 chicken (3 to 3½ pounds),
    cut into 8 pieces
1 large onion, cut into 1-inch
    chunks
2 celery stalks, cut into ½-inch
    chunks

1 tablespoon salt
½ teaspoon black pepper
7 medium-sized potatoes,
    peeled and cut in half
12 ounces bow-tie pasta

In an 8-quart soup pot, combine the water, chicken, onion, celery, salt, and pepper over medium-high heat and bring to a boil. Cover, reduce the heat to medium-low, and cook for 50 minutes. Remove the chicken to a platter, then add the potatoes to the pot and cook for 10 minutes. Add the pasta to the pot and cook for 8 to 10 minutes, or until the pasta is tender. Meanwhile, bone the chicken, discarding the bones and skin and cutting the meat into bite-sized pieces. Return the chicken to the pot and continue cooking until heated through. Serve in bowls.

NOTE: This will thicken up as it sits, so you may want to add additional water when you reheat any leftovers.

Traffic Light Pasta

4 to 6 servings

Stop! You'll want to *yield* to the fresh flavors in this red, yellow, and green dish before you *go* any farther!

12 ounces angel hair
(capellini) pasta
1½ boneless, skinless chicken
breasts, cut into thin strips
1 bottle (16 ounces) creamy
pepper-Parmesan salad
dressing
1 cup oil-packed sun-dried
tomatoes, drained and
thinly sliced

1 medium-sized yellow bell
pepper, cut into thin strips
1 package (10 ounces) frozen
asparagus spears, thawed
and cut in half

In a 6-quart soup pot, cook the pasta according to the package directions; drain, rinse, drain again, and set aside in the colander. Add the remaining ingredients to the pot and cook for 10 to 12 minutes over medium-high heat, or until no pink remains in the chicken, stirring frequently. Return the pasta to the pot and toss to coat; cook for 1 to 2 minutes, or until the pasta is heated through. Serve immediately.

NOTE: If you use sun-dried tomatoes that are not packed in oil, make sure to first soak them in water until softened.

Asian Chicken Linguine

I sure am partial to Asian-flavored chicken dishes, and with the flavors of garlic, ginger, and hoisin sauce, this one is a sure-fire passport to Asia!

1 pound linguine
3 tablespoons sesame oil
1½ pounds boneless, skinless
   chicken breasts, cut into
   thin strips
¾ pound fresh mushrooms,
   thinly sliced

3 garlic cloves, minced
¾ teaspoon ground ginger
½ teaspoon cayenne pepper
⅓ cup hoisin sauce (see Note)
3 tablespoons soy sauce
6 scallions, sliced diagonally

In a 6-quart soup pot, cook the pasta according to the package directions; drain, rinse, drain again, and set aside in the colander. In the same pot, heat the oil over medium heat, then add the chicken and sauté for 5 to 8 minutes, or until no pink remains, stirring constantly. Add the mushrooms, garlic, ginger, and cayenne pepper; cook for 5 minutes, stirring occasionally. Add the hoisin sauce and soy sauce, return the pasta to the pot, and toss until well coated. Cook for 2 to 3 minutes, or until the pasta is heated through. Add the sliced scallions, toss, and serve immediately.

NOTE: Hoisin sauce can usually be found next to the soy sauce in the ethnic food section of the supermarket.

Sautéed Chicken Livers and Pasta

6 to 8 servings

I first had this flavorful dish in a neighborhood Italian restaurant in Hoboken, New Jersey. You've gotta trust me and try it. . . . The taste is hearty Italian through and through.

1 pound linguine
½ cup (1 stick) butter
1 bay leaf
1 pound chicken livers, cut in half
1 large onion, chopped

1 teaspoon salt
½ teaspoon black pepper
1 jar (26 ounces) spaghetti sauce
1 package (10 ounces) frozen peas, thawed

In a 6-quart soup pot, cook the linguine according to the package directions; drain, rinse, drain again, and set aside in the colander. In the same pot, melt the butter over high heat. Add the bay leaf and stir constantly until the butter turns golden brown. Add the livers, onion, salt, and pepper. Cook for 10 to 12 minutes, or until the livers are no longer pink and the onions are tender, stirring frequently. Add the spaghetti sauce and cook for 2 to 3 minutes, or until bubbly. Add the peas and return the pasta to the pot, stirring until thoroughly combined. Cook for 3 to 5 minutes, or until heated through. **Be sure to remove the bay leaf before serving.**

NOTE: An old-fashioned butcher, or even some supermarkets, will still include all the parts when you buy a whole chicken, so you can freeze the livers until you have enough to make this recipe. Or you can buy chicken livers in a 1-pound package in the supermarket meat department.

Mediterranean Seafood Pasta

4 to 6 servings

Don't you love making dishes that originated in different places around the world? I sure do. We get to taste the flavors of a new place without leaving home. With this quick pasta dish, it's the feta cheese, olives, and shrimp that bring a touch of Greece right to our tables.

12 ounces angel hair
(capellini) pasta
2 tablespoons olive oil
1 medium-sized red onion,
chopped
¼ cup red wine vinegar
3 tablespoons lemon juice
2 teaspoons garlic powder
1 pound large shrimp, peeled
and deveined, but tails
left on (see Note)

1 can (28 ounces) whole
tomatoes, drained and
quartered
1 can (2¼ ounces) sliced black
olives, drained
2 tablespoons dried oregano
1 teaspoon black pepper
1 cup (4 ounces) crumbled feta
cheese

In a 6-quart soup pot, cook the pasta according to the package directions; drain, rinse, drain again, and set aside in the colander. In the same pot, heat the oil over medium-high heat and sauté the onion for 4 to 5 minutes, or until tender. Add the vinegar, lemon juice, garlic powder, and shrimp; cook for 3 to 4 minutes, or until the shrimp are cooked through and pink. Add the tomatoes, olives, oregano, and pepper. Return the pasta to the pot and heat, stirring until thoroughly mixed and warmed through. Sprinkle with the feta cheese and serve.

NOTE: I like to leave the tails on the shrimp because they look better that way, but you can certainly take them off if you'd rather make them easier to eat.

The Skillet

A Range of Stovetop Winners

Whether you know these as skillets, frying pans, or sauté pans, they're all pretty much the same thing—low pans with tapered or straight sides in size range from 6 inches to 12 inches. In this chapter, we use 10- to 12-inch skillets.

Which materials work the best? Should your skillet be stainless steel, copper, aluminum, cast iron, or glass? Many people have specific favorites, and it's up to you to decide which specific cooking pans you prefer. But if you're in the market for some new ones, my suggestion is to get skillets with a nonreactive metal surface so you can cook any type of food in them. Many pans have heat channels or are constructed in several layers to accomplish even heat distribution—and even heat is ideal. As for nonstick or coated pans, use ones that have a durable cooking surface.

Keep these points in mind:

- Be certain to use the proper-size pan—a skillet that's too big may burn food and one that's too small may get you a messy stovetop!

- Be sure the handles of your pans are tight. Many pan handles tend to loosen over time but can be tightened simply with a screwdriver. Check your handles and play it safe.

113

- When it comes to lids, you want ones that fit properly. So if a recipe calls for a covered skillet, make sure that you have one with a snug-fitting lid so your dish will cook properly.

- If serving dinner directly from the pan, don't forget the trivet, so you won't burn your counter or tabletop.

The Skillet

A Range of Stovetop Winners

Greek Beef and Mushroom Orzo

4 servings

Serve your family this Greek mushroom steak with delicate orzo pasta and feta cheese, and you'll be hailed as a god or goddess of the kitchen!

2 tablespoons olive oil
1 pound boneless beef top
    sirloin steak, cut into
    ¼-inch slices across the
    grain
1 pound fresh mushrooms, cut
    into ½-inch slices
1 can (14½ ounces) Italian
    stewed tomatoes

1 can (14½ ounces) ready-to-
    use chicken broth
½ cup water
¼ teaspoon dried oregano
¼ teaspoon dried basil
8 ounces orzo pasta
⅔ cup crumbled feta cheese

In a large skillet, heat the oil over high heat. Add the steak and brown for 5 to 6 minutes; drain off the fat. Add the mushrooms and cook for 6 to 8 minutes, or just until they begin to brown. Add the tomatoes, chicken broth, water, oregano, basil, and orzo. Bring to a boil, then reduce the heat to low, cover, and simmer for 8 to 9 minutes, or until the orzo is tender. Stir in the cheese and serve immediately.

Skillet Pepper Steak

4 servings

When you want to impress without a big mess, peppers and steak are just what to make!

3 tablespoons olive oil, divided
4 medium-sized potatoes,
    peeled and thinly sliced
½ teaspoon salt
¼ teaspoon black pepper
1 pound boneless beef chuck
    steak, very thinly sliced

2 garlic cloves, minced
1 large green bell pepper, cut
    into ¼-inch strips
2 tablespoons soy sauce

In a large skillet, heat 2 tablespoons oil over medium-high heat. Add the potatoes and sprinkle with the salt and black pepper. Sauté for 12 to 15 minutes, or until golden, turning halfway through the cooking. Remove to a platter and cover to keep warm. Add the remaining 1 tablespoon oil to the skillet, then add the steak, garlic, and bell pepper. Increase the heat to high and sauté for 4 to 5 minutes, or until the steak is cooked. Add the soy sauce and stir to coat. Cook for 1 minute, then spoon the steak and pepper mixture over the potatoes.

Chunky Garden Sloppy Joes

6 servings

It's not always easy to make sure we serve enough veggies with our meals, but this new garden-fresh twist on an old favorite is a guaranteed "good-for-you"!

1½ pounds ground beef
1 large zucchini, chopped
1 medium-sized onion,
  chopped

1 large tomato, chopped
1 jar (26 ounces) spaghetti
  sauce
6 hamburger buns, split

In a large skillet, brown the ground beef, zucchini, and onion over medium-high heat for 10 to 12 minutes, or until no pink remains in the beef and the zucchini is tender. Reduce the heat to medium-low and stir in the tomato and spaghetti sauce. Cook for 4 to 5 minutes, or until heated through. Spoon over the buns and serve immediately.

Beefy Rice Pie

4 to 6 servings

After a hectic day, we all look forward to a home-cooked meal. And when we're the ones doing the cooking, nothing beats this saucy beef and rice pie that makes short work in the kitchen!

1 pound ground beef
½ pound hot or sweet Italian
    pork sausage, casings
    removed
1 can (8 ounces) tomato sauce
2 cups cooked rice

4 slices (6 ounces total)
    mozzarella cheese
2 tablespoons grated
    Parmesan cheese

In a large skillet, brown the ground beef and sausage for 8 to 10 minutes over medium-high heat until crumbly and no pink remains; drain off the excess liquid, remove to a medium-sized bowl, and set aside. In another medium-sized bowl, combine the tomato sauce and rice, then spread half the mixture in the skillet. Top with half of the meat mixture, then place 2 slices mozzarella cheese over the top and sprinkle with 1 tablespoon Parmesan cheese. Repeat the layers. Cover and cook over medium-low heat for 8 to 10 minutes, or until the cheese melts. Let sit for 5 minutes, then slice into wedges and serve immediately.

NOTE: Go ahead and give it a sprinkle of fresh chopped parsley or paprika for a little added color.

All-in-One Pierogi Skillet

4 servings

Wow! Ground beef and broccoli never had it so good, 'cause now they're teamed with puffy, melt-in-your-mouth, everybody-loves-'em potato pierogis. Better make extra!

1 tablespoon vegetable oil
1 pound ground beef
1 package (16 ounces) frozen
    potato pierogis, thawed
1 package (10 ounces) frozen
    broccoli florets, thawed

½ teaspoon salt
¼ teaspoon black pepper
1 cup (4 ounces) shredded
    Cheddar cheese

In a large skillet, heat the oil over medium-high heat and brown the beef for 5 minutes, stirring frequently. Add the pierogis and cook for 4 to 5 minutes, or until heated through. Stir in the broccoli, salt, and pepper, then top with the cheese. Reduce the heat to low, cover, and cook for 2 to 3 minutes, or until the cheese is melted and the broccoli is warmed through.

Down-home Liver 'n' Onions

If you quiver at the thought of liver, please do me (and yourself) a favor and try this home-style version. Loaded with tasty whole new potatoes, it may just change your point of view!

2 tablespoons vegetable oil
5 medium-sized onions, cut
   into wedges
1½ pounds beef liver, cut into
   ¾-inch strips

2 cans (14½ ounces each)
   whole potatoes, drained
   and cut in half
½ teaspoon salt
½ teaspoon black pepper

In a large skillet, heat the oil over medium-high heat and sauté the onions for 8 to 10 minutes, or until tender and just beginning to brown. Add the liver and cook for 8 minutes, stirring occasionally. Stir in the remaining ingredients; cook for 6 to 8 minutes, or until the potatoes are heated through and the liver is cooked to desired doneness.

Greek Island Frittata

6 to 8 servings

Even though a frittata is a "loaded" omelet, it's still pretty easy to make. So if you like to keep things simple, and if you like dishes with a foreign flair, this one's for you!

1 pound ground lamb
¼ cup olive oil
3 cups Tater Tots® (about ⅓ of a 2-pound package)
1 dozen eggs
1 package (10 ounces) frozen chopped spinach, thawed and drained

1 cup (4 ounces) crumbled feta cheese
½ teaspoon dried oregano
½ teaspoon salt

In a 12-inch nonstick skillet, brown the lamb over high heat for 5 to 6 minutes; drain off the excess liquid, place the lamb in a medium-sized bowl, and set aside. In the same skillet, heat the oil over high heat; add the Tater Tots® and cook for 8 to 10 minutes, or until golden brown, stirring occasionally. Meanwhile, in a large bowl, whisk together the eggs, spinach, cheese, oregano, and salt until well mixed. Pour over the Tater Tots® and reduce the heat to low. Cook for 8 to 10 minutes, tilting the pan occasionally, until the eggs are almost set. Sprinkle with the lamb, cover, and cook until completely set. Cut into wedges and serve.

Magical Pineapple Pork Chops

4 servings

It's magic! Know why? Pineapple chunks and sweet yams make this a real disappearing act. And you get to take all the bows!

¼ cup all-purpose flour
¼ teaspoon salt
⅛ teaspoon black pepper
4 pork loin chops (1¼ to 1½ pounds total), ¾ inch thick
2 tablespoons vegetable oil
1 can (8¼ ounces) pineapple chunks in heavy syrup, drained and syrup reserved

1 tablespoon light brown sugar
¼ teaspoon ground cinnamon
1 can (29 ounces) yams, drained and cut into 1-inch chunks

In a shallow dish, combine the flour, salt, and pepper. Completely coat the pork chops in the flour mixture. In a large deep skillet, heat the oil over medium-high heat and brown the pork chops for 10 minutes, turning halfway through the cooking. In a small bowl, combine the reserved pineapple syrup, the brown sugar, and cinnamon; pour over the chops and stir until the sauce is thickened. Reduce the heat to low, turn the chops over, and add the pineapple chunks and yams to the skillet. Cover and simmer for 10 to 12 minutes, or until the yams are warmed through.

Deviled Ham Skillet

4 to 6 servings

They're sure to see a devilish gleam in your eye when you proudly serve wedges of this hearty skillet treat. With its perfect teaming of deviled ham, cheese, veggies, and rice, you're gonna shine!

1 medium-sized onion, finely chopped
3 celery stalks, chopped
2 cans (7 ounces each) sliced mushrooms, drained
2 cans (4½ ounces each) deviled ham
3 cups cooked rice
6 eggs, beaten
2 cups (8 ounces) shredded Cheddar cheese
1 can (3 ounces) real bacon bits

Coat a large skillet with nonstick vegetable spray and sauté the onion and celery over medium heat for 4 to 5 minutes, or until tender. Stir in the mushrooms, ham, and rice. Pour the eggs evenly over the rice mixture, then reduce the heat to low, cover, and cook for 18 to 20 minutes, or until the eggs are set. Uncover and sprinkle with the cheese. Cook for 3 to 4 minutes, or until the cheese melts. Sprinkle the bacon bits evenly over the top, then slice into wedges and serve immediately.

Sausage-Stuffed Bread Bowl

4 to 6 servings

Some foods are so good that we're tempted to lick the bowl. Well, with this one, we get to eat it!

¼ cup vegetable oil
4 medium-sized bell peppers
    (2 red and 2 green), cut
    into ½-inch strips
2 large onions, cut into ¼-inch
    slices

1 loaf (1 pound) Italian bread
1½ pounds hot or sweet
    Italian pork sausage, cut
    into 2-inch pieces
2 cups spaghetti sauce

In a large skillet, heat the oil over medium-high heat and sauté the peppers and onions for 12 to 15 minutes, or until the onions are golden, stirring occasionally; remove to a bowl and set aside. Meanwhile, slice ½ inch off the top of the bread and set it aside; pull out the center of the bread and save it for another use. In the same skillet, cook the sausage for 12 to 15 minutes over medium-high heat, or until no pink remains. Return the onions and peppers to the skillet, then add the spaghetti sauce; mix well. Cook for 3 to 5 minutes, or until thoroughly heated. Spoon into the center of the bread, replace the top and, using a serrated knife, slice into individual servings.

Egg Foo Yung

3 to 4 servings

How many times have you had this at a Chinese restaurant and wondered why you've never made it at home? Well, now you can! And wait till you see how fast you can whip it up yourself.

8 eggs
1 can (4 ounces) sliced
  mushrooms, drained and
  coarsely chopped
½ pound fresh bean sprouts,
  coarsely chopped
¼ pound thick-sliced deli roast
  pork, coarsely chopped

3 scallions, thinly sliced
¼ teaspoon salt
¼ teaspoon black pepper
About ¼ cup peanut oil
1 can (10½ ounces) chicken
  gravy
2 teaspoons soy sauce
1 teaspoon ground ginger

In a large bowl, beat the eggs. Add the mushrooms, bean sprouts, pork, scallions, salt, and pepper; mix well and set aside. Heat 1 tablespoon oil in a large nonstick skillet over high heat. Spoon three ¼-cup measures of the egg mixture into the skillet to form "pancakes" and cook for about 2 minutes, or until golden brown, turning halfway through the cooking. Remove to a serving platter and cover to keep warm. Repeat until all of the egg mixture has been cooked, adding more oil to the skillet as needed. Combine the gravy, soy sauce, and ginger in the skillet; mix well. Heat over medium heat for 1 minute, or until warmed through. Serve the gravy over the pancakes.

NOTE: Ask the deli at your supermarket to slice the roast pork into thick slices. Then you can chop them coarsely to get good-sized chunks of pork in your pancakes.

Jazzy Jambalaya

4 to 6 servings

Me-oh-my-oh, the best part of this jazzy concoction is that it makes you feel like you're down on the bayou. Have some fun!

½ pound bacon
1 large onion, chopped
1 medium-sized green bell pepper, chopped
½ cup uncooked long-grain rice
1½ pounds boneless, skinless chicken breasts, cut into ½-inch chunks

1 pound kielbasa sausage, cut into ½-inch slices
1 can (14½ ounces) ready-to-use chicken broth
1 can (8 ounces) tomato sauce
⅛ teaspoon black pepper
1 pound large shrimp, peeled and deveined, but tails left on

In a large skillet, cook the bacon over medium heat for 7 to 8 minutes, or until crisp and brown. Remove to a paper towel to drain, then crumble and set aside. Add the onion, bell pepper, and rice to the bacon drippings in the pan and cook for 8 to 10 minutes, or until the rice is golden, stirring frequently; remove to a medium-sized bowl and set aside. Increase the heat under the skillet to high and cook the chicken and sausage for 8 to 10 minutes, or until the chicken begins to brown. Return the rice mixture to the skillet and add the chicken broth, tomato sauce, and black pepper; mix well, then bring to a boil. Reduce the heat to low, cover, and simmer for 20 to 25 minutes, or until the rice is tender. Add the shrimp and bacon; cover and cook for 5 minutes, or until the shrimp are pink and cooked through.

127

Arroz con Pollo

4 to 6 servings

Arroz con pollo may be Spanish for "chicken with rice," but it really means so much more because of the extra touches we add. And, skin on or skin off, this tender chicken is going to bring loads of smiles to your dinner table!

½ cup all-purpose flour
1 chicken (3 to 3½ pounds),
 cut into 8 pieces
2 tablespoons olive oil
1 medium-sized onion,
 chopped
2 large celery stalks, sliced
2 cups water

1 can (8 ounces) tomato sauce
½ teaspoon paprika
1 teaspoon salt
½ teaspoon black pepper
1 cup uncooked long-
 grain rice
1 package (10 ounces) frozen
 peas, thawed

Place the flour in a large resealable plastic storage bag. Add the chicken and shake until thoroughly coated. In a large deep skillet, heat the oil over medium-high heat. Add the chicken, onion, and celery, and cook for 15 minutes, turning the chicken occasionally to brown evenly. Add the water, tomato sauce, paprika, salt, and pepper; bring to a boil. Add the rice and stir until completely coated with the sauce. Reduce the heat to low, cover, and simmer for 25 to 30 minutes, or until the rice is tender. Add the peas, cover, and cook for 3 to 5 minutes, or until the peas are heated through.

NOTE: If I have the time, I like to remove the skin from the chicken before cooking to reduce the amount of fat.

Stovetop Chicken Noodle Parmigiana

4 servings

Keep the kitchen cool with this stovetop version of a classic Italian dish. And this time it's made with oodles and oodles of ramen noodles!

1 egg, beaten
½ cup Italian-flavored bread
    crumbs
4 boneless, skinless chicken
    breast halves (1 to 1½
    pounds total)
¼ cup vegetable oil
1 jar (26 ounces) spaghetti
    sauce

1½ cups water
½ pound fresh mushrooms,
    cut in half
2 packages (3 ounces each)
    ramen noodles, broken up
½ cup (2 ounces) shredded
    mozzarella cheese

Place the egg in a shallow dish. Place the bread crumbs in another shallow dish. Dip the chicken in the egg, then in the bread crumbs, coating completely. In a large skillet, heat the oil over medium-high heat. Cook the chicken for 5 to 6 minutes, or until no pink remains, turning halfway through the cooking. Remove the chicken to a serving platter and cover to keep warm. Add the remaining ingredients except the cheese to the skillet (reserve the seasoning packets from the noodles for another use). Cook for 4 to 5 minutes, or until the noodles are tender. Reduce the heat to medium-low and return the chicken to the skillet, placing it over the noodles. Sprinkle the chicken with the mozzarella cheese. Cover and cook for 4 to 5 minutes, or until the cheese is melted and the chicken is warmed through.

129

Chinese Chicken Roll-ups

5 servings

So many ways to cook chicken . . . so little time . . . and when it sounds complicated, should we even try it? You'd better try *these*! They're a cinch to make 'cause all the ingredients get cooked in one pan, then spooned into flour tortillas for no-fuss serving.

¼ cup sesame oil

1½ pounds boneless, skinless chicken breasts, cut into 1-inch pieces

3 garlic cloves, minced

1 package (8 ounces) coleslaw mix (shredded cabbage and carrots)

1 can (14 ounces) bean sprouts, drained

1 can (8 ounces) sliced water chestnuts, drained

⅓ cup hoisin sauce

⅓ cup soy sauce

¼ cup firmly packed light brown sugar

1 tablespoon cornstarch

1 can (5 ounces) chow mein noodles

Ten 8-inch flour tortillas, warmed

In a large skillet, heat 2 tablespoons oil over medium-high heat and brown the chicken and garlic for 8 to 10 minutes. Add the coleslaw mix, bean sprouts, and water chestnuts; cook for 4 to 5 minutes, or until the cabbage and carrots are tender. In a small bowl, combine the hoisin sauce, soy sauce, brown sugar, cornstarch, and the remaining 2 tablespoons sesame oil. Pour over the chicken mixture and bring to a boil. Add the noodles and stir until thoroughly mixed and warmed through. Spoon onto the tortillas, roll up jelly-roll style, and serve.

NOTE: You can spread extra hoisin sauce on the tortillas before filling, if you'd like.

Philly Chicken Subs

6 servings

Chicken with all the fixin's makes a great *sub*-stitute for steak in these hot and filling sandwiches.

1 tablespoon vegetable oil
2 large onions, thinly sliced
½ pound fresh mushrooms, sliced
½ teaspoon salt
¼ teaspoon black pepper
1½ pounds boneless, skinless chicken breasts, cut into thin strips
1 cup (4 ounces) shredded Cheddar cheese
6 hoagie rolls, split

In a large nonstick skillet, heat the oil over high heat. Add the onions, mushrooms, salt, and pepper and cook for 8 to 10 minutes, or until the onions are golden. Remove from the skillet and set aside. In the same skillet, cook the chicken for 6 to 8 minutes, or until no pink remains, stirring frequently. Return the onions and mushrooms to the skillet and cook for 3 to 5 more minutes, or until thoroughly combined and warmed through. Sprinkle with the cheese, cover, and cook until the cheese melts. Place the mixture on the hoagie rolls and serve.

NOTE: You can use hot sauce, ketchup, or the condiment of your choice on these great sandwiches. In Philly, a sauce made of pasteurized-process cheese spread (such as Velveeta®) is the most popular, so feel free to replace the Cheddar cheese with that, if you'd like.

Chicken-Walnut Skillet Pie

4 to 6 servings

Perfect for company or for the family, this pie is made with a savory walnut stuffing that adds just the right flavor and texture to everyday chicken.

¼ cup (½ stick) butter
1 cup shredded zucchini
⅔ cup water
2 cups herb-seasoned
    stuffing mix
1 tablespoon vegetable oil
1½ pounds boneless, skinless
    chicken breasts, cut into
    1-inch chunks

¼ teaspoon salt
⅛ teaspoon black pepper
3 eggs, beaten
1 can (5 ounces) evaporated
    milk
½ cup chopped walnuts,
    divided
1 cup (4 ounces) shredded
    sharp Cheddar cheese

In a large skillet, melt the butter over medium-high heat and sauté the zucchini for 3 minutes. Add the water and stuffing mix and stir until thoroughly combined. Remove to a large bowl and set aside. Heat the oil in the same skillet over medium-high heat and add the chicken; sprinkle with the salt and pepper and sauté for 3 to 5 minutes until no pink remains. Drain off the excess liquid. Meanwhile, in a medium-sized bowl, combine the eggs, evaporated milk, and ¼ cup walnuts. Pour over the chicken and sprinkle with the cheese. Cover with the stuffing mixture and sprinkle the remaining ¼ cup walnuts over the top. Reduce the heat to low, cover, and cook for 8 to 10 minutes, or until set. Cut into wedges and serve.

Standout Skillet Chicken Cacciatore

6 servings

Take the ho-hum out of chicken with a sauce that makes it stand out from the crowd. When it's served over pasta or rice, you really get to savor the flavor, too!

¼ cup all-purpose flour
1 teaspoon salt
½ teaspoon black pepper
6 boneless, skinless chicken
    breast halves (1½ to 2
    pounds total)
2 tablespoons olive oil
1 medium-sized onion, cut in
    half and thinly sliced

2 medium-sized green bell
    peppers, cut into thin
    strips
½ pound fresh mushrooms,
    sliced
1 jar (26 ounces) spaghetti
    sauce

In a shallow dish, combine the flour, salt, and pepper. Coat the chicken with the flour mixture. In a large skillet, heat the oil over medium heat and brown the chicken breasts for 5 to 7 minutes, turning halfway through the cooking. Add the remaining ingredients, stirring to combine, then reduce the heat to medium-low, cover, and simmer for 30 minutes to allow the flavors to "marry."

The Casserole Dish

All Mixed Up

No matter if you're headed to a potluck supper or to your own kitchen table, casseroles are the perfect choice. For years, casseroles have been a popular meal choice, and with our desire for more and more convenience these days, casseroles still offer us a tasty answer.

In most cases, casseroles are combinations of meats, vegetables, and starches with a few seasonings. They get popped into the oven and that's it for us—we let the oven do the rest!

I've got a few ways to make these "easies" even easier:

- Choose the proper-size casserole dish. One that's too large will give you a dried-out casserole. And one that's too small may cause your casserole to bubble up and overflow, making quite a mess in the oven!

- Place a rimmed baking sheet under a casserole dish just in case a full casserole overflows.

- Many casseroles can be assembled and frozen before cooking, then thawed in the refrigerator and baked according to recipe instructions. Now that's what I call a real time-saver! (Some dishes may need a bit more baking time. Check to be sure it's thoroughly heated.)

- Today's casserole dish selection is almost unlimited. Glass, porcelain, earthenware, patterned, colored . . . they're all perfect for putting your baked concoction right on even the fanciest dinner table.

- Always place a trivet or hot pad under a hot casserole dish to prevent scorching counters and tabletops.

The Casserole Dish
All Mixed Up

Beef Burgundy Casserole

4 to 6 servings

When I really wanna turn some heads, I fix this fancy-sounding beef dish. The rich sauce bowls them over every time, so nobody ever believes how super-simple it is!

2½ cups water
1½ cups Burgundy or other
    dry red wine
1 can (10¾ ounces) condensed
    golden mushroom soup
2 pounds boneless beef top
    sirloin steak, trimmed and
    cut into 1-inch cubes

1 package (6 ounces)
    uncooked long-grain and
    wild rice mix with
    seasoning packet

Preheat the oven to 375°F. In a 5-quart casserole dish, combine the water, wine, mushroom soup, steak, and the seasoning packet from the rice mix; mix well. Cover and bake for 30 minutes. Remove from the oven and stir in the rice mix. Cover and bake for 60 to 70 minutes, or until the rice is tender.

Double-Delight Pineapple-Ham Bake

6 servings

This is really two treats in one. Made according to these directions, it's a tasty main course dish. Leave out the ham, and it's a sweet pineapple bread pudding that's super for dessert. Try it both ways!

One 1½-pound fully cooked boneless ham, cut into 6 slices
6 slices white bread, cut into 1-inch cubes
6 eggs, beaten

1 can (20 ounces) crushed pineapple in syrup, undrained
1 cup sugar
½ cup (1 stick) butter, softened

Preheat the oven to 375°F. Place the ham slices evenly in the bottom of a 9" × 13" baking dish that has been coated with nonstick vegetable spray. In a large bowl, combine the remaining ingredients; mix well and pour over the ham slices. Bake, uncovered, for 45 to 50 minutes, or until the top is golden.

Scalloped Potatoes and Ham

4 to 6 servings

There's more than one way to be a ham. And when you want to please the gang and take all the credit yourself, this creamy fill-them-up hit will win you loads of raves.

¾ pound fully cooked boneless ham, cut into ½-inch chunks

1 package (26 ounces) frozen shredded hash brown potatoes, thawed

2 cans (10¾ ounces each) condensed cream of celery soup

1 package (10 ounces) frozen peas

1½ cups milk

¼ teaspoon black pepper

Preheat the oven to 350°F. In a large bowl, combine all the ingredients; mix well. Pour into a 9" × 13" baking dish that has been coated with nonstick vegetable spray and cover tightly with aluminum foil. Bake for 30 minutes, then uncover and bake for 50 to 60 more minutes, or until the potatoes are tender and the top is golden.

Deviled Ham Soufflé

4 to 6 servings

With this soufflé, you'll be able to rise to any occasion, 'cause it's down-home delicious and sinfully easy!

8 eggs, beaten
6 onion rolls, cut into 1-inch
    chunks
1 small onion, finely chopped
1 small green bell pepper,
    finely chopped

2 cans (4¼ ounces each)
    deviled ham
1 can (10¾ ounces) condensed
    cream of mushroom soup
1½ cups milk
1 teaspoon dry mustard

In a large bowl, combine all the ingredients; mix well. Pour into a 9" × 13" baking dish that has been coated with non-stick vegetable spray. Bake, uncovered, for 40 to 45 minutes, or until a knife inserted in the center comes out clean and the soufflé is golden brown.

State Fair Tortellini

4 to 6 servings

Worthy of top prize at any state fair, this "pocket pasta" dish, smothered in a robust sauce full of chunky veggies and cheese, will make you look like a winning chef right in your own home.

1 jar (26 ounces) spaghetti sauce

2 packages (9 ounces each) Italian sausage–filled fresh or frozen (thawed) tortellini (see Note)

1½ cups water

1 large green bell pepper, cut into 1-inch chunks

1 medium-sized onion, cut into thin wedges

1 can (4 ounces) mushrooms, drained

2 cups (8 ounces) shredded mozzarella cheese

Preheat the oven to 350°F. In a 9" × 13" baking dish, combine all the ingredients except the cheese; mix well. Cover tightly with aluminum foil. Bake for 25 minutes; remove from the oven, stir, cover, and return to the oven for 20 more minutes. Remove the foil and sprinkle with the cheese. Return to the oven and bake, uncovered, for 5 more minutes, or until the cheese is melted.

NOTE: Fresh tortellini can usually be found in the refrigerated section of your grocery store, near the dairy foods.

Hot Dog Bundles

6 servings

They'll be shouting "Hot diggity dog!" for this combo of hot dogs and beans served together in buns.

1 pound hot dogs, cut into
  1-inch pieces
2 cans (16 ounces each)
  vegetarian baked beans
1 small onion, minced
½ cup firmly packed light
  brown sugar

½ cup chili sauce
1 tablespoon cider vinegar
1 teaspoon prepared yellow
  mustard
6 hot dog rolls, split

Preheat the oven to 350°F. In a 2-quart casserole dish, combine all the ingredients except the buns; mix well. Cover and bake for 45 to 50 minutes, or until hot and bubbly. Spoon into the hot dog buns and serve.

Baked Sausage Ravioli

4 to 6 servings

There are so many different pasta types and shapes today that we could surely make a new dish every night and almost never run out of variations. I bet you haven't tried this one yet—it's made with sausage-stuffed ravioli in a tomato-cheese sauce and it goes together in no time.

1 can (10¾ ounces) condensed Cheddar cheese soup
1 cup milk
1 package (10 ounces) frozen chopped broccoli, thawed
1 jar (26 ounces) spaghetti sauce

2 packages (9 ounces each) Italian sausage–filled fresh or frozen (thawed) ravioli (see Note)
2 tablespoons grated Parmesan cheese

Preheat the oven to 375°F. In a large bowl, combine all the ingredients except the Parmesan cheese; spoon into a 9" × 13" baking dish that has been coated with nonstick vegetable spray. Cover with aluminum foil and bake for 50 minutes. Remove the foil and bake for 8 to 10 more minutes, or until the top is set. Sprinkle with the Parmesan cheese and serve.

NOTE: Fresh ravioli can usually be found in the refrigerated section of your grocery store, near the dairy foods.

Crunchy Turkey Bake

4 to 6 servings

They're bound to gobble this dish right down, 'cause it's the perfect team of creamy and crunchy!

1 pound deli turkey, cut into ½-inch cubes (see Note)
2 cans (15 ounces each) mixed vegetables, drained (see Note)
1 can (10¾ ounces) condensed cream of mushroom soup
1 can (8 ounces) sliced water chestnuts, drained

1 cup (4 ounces) shredded sharp Cheddar cheese
¾ cup mayonnaise
1 medium-sized onion, finely chopped
3 celery stalks, finely chopped
1 cup coarsely crushed cheese-flavored crackers

Preheat the oven to 350°F. In a large bowl, combine all the ingredients except the cracker crumbs; mix well. Spoon into a 3-quart casserole dish that has been coated with nonstick vegetable spray. Cover and bake for 60 minutes. Uncover and sprinkle the cracker crumbs over the top. Bake for 15 to 20 more minutes, or until bubbly and heated through.

NOTE: At your deli, ask that the turkey be cut into two ½-inch slices. That'll make it a snap for you to cut it into cubes. The canned mixed vegetables I like to use include carrots, potatoes, celery, sweet peas, green beans, corn, and lima beans all in one can.

Golden Chicken Casserole

4 to 6 servings

I always try to keep some biscuit baking mix on hand for stretching my food budget and making the most of leftovers. Take this dish . . . with yesterday's chicken and some Cheddar cheese, we can get a golden-crusted meal fit for a king!

1 can (10¾ ounces) condensed cream of chicken soup
½ cup sour cream
1¼ cups milk, divided
3 cups diced cooked chicken
1 package (16 ounces) frozen mixed vegetables
½ teaspoon salt
¼ teaspoon black pepper
¾ cup biscuit baking mix
¼ cup cornmeal
1 egg
2 cups (8 ounces) shredded Cheddar cheese

Preheat the oven to 375°F. In a 9" × 13" baking dish, combine the soup, sour cream, and ½ cup milk; mix well. Add the chicken, vegetables, salt, and pepper; mix well. In a medium-sized bowl, combine the baking mix, cornmeal, egg, and the remaining ¾ cup milk; mix well, then spoon over the chicken mixture. Sprinkle with the cheese and bake for 30 to 35 minutes, or until the edges are golden and the casserole is warmed through.

NOTE: To lighten this recipe a little, you can substitute reduced-fat soup, sour cream, and/or milk for the "regular" ingredient.

Pierogi Chicken Bake

4 to 6 servings

I let the supermarket freezer section help me out with this full-flavored casserole that goes together in a snap.

1½ pounds boneless, skinless
   chicken breasts, cut into
   ¼-inch strips
2 cans (12 ounces each)
   chicken gravy
1 package (16 ounces) frozen
   potato pierogis, thawed

1 package (10 ounces) frozen
   mixed vegetables
½ teaspoon salt
½ teaspoon black pepper
1 can (2.8 ounces) French-fried
   onions

Preheat the oven to 350°F. In a 9" × 13" baking dish, combine all the ingredients except the French-fried onions; stir gently until well combined. Cover with aluminum foil and bake for 50 minutes. Remove from the oven, uncover, and top with the French-fried onions. Bake for 5 more minutes, uncovered, or until the onions are golden brown.

New-fashioned Chicken Pot Pie

4 to 6 servings

I love to find new ways of making my old standbys, since there's no reason to fuss if we don't have to. Nope! And for this one, all we have to do is pick up some refrigerated crescent rolls and, like magic, we get old-fashioned pot pie that's new-fashioned easy!

2 cans (15 ounces each) mixed vegetables, drained
2 cans (10¾ ounces each) condensed cream of potato soup
1 cup milk
1 can (10 ounces) chunk white chicken, drained and flaked
½ teaspoon onion powder
¼ teaspoon salt
½ teaspoon black pepper
1 container (8 ounces) refrigerated crescent rolls

Preheat the oven to 400°F. In a large bowl, combine all the ingredients except the crescent rolls; mix well. Pour into a 9-inch deep-dish pie plate that has been coated with nonstick vegetable spray. Bake for 20 minutes, or until bubbly and hot. Meanwhile, separate the crescent rolls into 8 triangles. Beginning at the wide end, roll up each triangle halfway. Place the triangles over the baked chicken mixture, with the wide ends touching the outside rim of the pie plate and the pointed ends meeting in the center of the pie, spacing them evenly. Bake for 12 to 18 minutes, or until the crust is golden brown.

Tuna Rice Casserole

4 to 6 servings

Everyone I know loves tuna, so I'm always looking for new ways to make it special. I sure found it with this no-fuss dish of tender rice and crispy French-fried onions.

2 cans (10¾ ounces each) condensed cream of mushroom soup
1½ cups milk
½ cup water
1 tablespoon butter
½ teaspoon black pepper
2 cans (6 ounces each) tuna, drained and flaked
1 package (10 ounces) frozen peas
1½ cups uncooked long-grain parboiled white rice (see Note)
1 can (2.8 ounces) French-fried onions

Preheat the oven to 350°F. In a 2½-quart casserole dish, combine the soup, milk, water, butter, and pepper; mix well. Stir in the tuna, peas, and rice. Cover and bake for 1 hour and 15 minutes. Uncover and top with the French-fried onions; bake for 5 to 7 more minutes, or until the onions are golden and the casserole is bubbly.

NOTE: Long-grain parboiled white rice, also known as Converted rice, can usually be found in the supermarket rice section. Be sure your rice is tender before topping the casserole with the French-fried onions.

Caesar-Baked Ravioli

4 to 5 servings

Just because this is named "Caesar" doesn't mean it has to be a salad. Noooo! But when we take that popular Caesar taste and combine it with something unexpected, we get two surprises in one!

1 can (10¾ ounces) condensed cream of mushroom soup
¾ cup milk
½ cup sour cream
1 envelope (1.2 ounces) dry Caesar salad dressing mix
1 package (25 ounces) frozen cheese ravioli, thawed
1 package (9 ounces) frozen Italian green beans, thawed and drained
¼ cup Italian-flavored bread crumbs

Preheat the oven to 350°F. In a large bowl, combine the soup, milk, sour cream, and Caesar dressing mix; mix well. Gently stir in the ravioli and green beans until well combined. Pour into a 7" × 11" baking dish that has been coated with nonstick vegetable spray; sprinkle with the bread crumbs. Cover tightly with aluminum foil and bake for 50 minutes, then uncover and bake for 5 to 7 more minutes, or until the bread crumbs are golden.

Spinach and Bacon Quiche

4 to 6 servings

It shouldn't be hard to get them to eat their spinach when it's mixed into this light-as-a-feather cheesy pie filled with crunchy bits of bacon. What *will* be hard to do is to make sure they save some for you!

1 cup (4 ounces) shredded
    Cheddar cheese
1 cup (4 ounces) shredded
    Swiss cheese
1 unbaked frozen 9-inch pie
    shell, thawed
½ cup real bacon bits
1 package (10 ounces) frozen
    chopped spinach, thawed,
    drained, and squeezed dry

2 eggs
1 cup milk
1 teaspoon onion powder
¼ teaspoon white pepper
¼ teaspoon ground nutmeg

Preheat the oven to 350°F. In a medium-sized bowl, combine the Cheddar and Swiss cheeses; sprinkle half the mixture over the bottom of the pie shell. Sprinkle the bacon bits over the cheese and top with the spinach, then the remaining cheese. In the same bowl, combine the eggs, milk, onion powder, and pepper; beat until thoroughly mixed. Pour into the pie shell; sprinkle with the nutmeg. Bake for 40 to 45 minutes, or until the filling is set. Remove from the oven and cool on a wire rack for 5 minutes before cutting and serving.

Snazzy Salmon and Artichoke Quiche

4 to 6 servings

Quiche is just a fancy way to say cheese pie. But when we dress it up with artichoke hearts and canned salmon, suddenly it's got real pizzazz!

2 cups (8 ounces) shredded
  Italian cheese blend
1 unbaked frozen 9-inch deep-
  dish pie shell, thawed
1 can (14 ounces) artichoke
  hearts, drained well and
  chopped

1 can (7½ ounces) red salmon,
  skin and bones removed,
  flaked
1 small onion, finely chopped
2 eggs
1 cup milk
¼ teaspoon white pepper

Preheat the oven to 350°F. Sprinkle half of the cheese over the bottom of the pie shell. Spread the artichoke hearts evenly over the cheese and top with the salmon and onion, then the remaining cheese. In a medium-sized bowl, combine the eggs, milk, and pepper; beat until thoroughly mixed, then pour into the pie shell. Bake for 40 to 45 minutes, or until the filling is set. Remove from the oven and cool on a wire rack for 5 minutes before cutting and serving.

Roasting Pans and Baking Dishes

Oven-to-Table Meals

Let's talk "hearty." I mean real "sink your teeth into them" meals. Don't worry—I'll have you out of the kitchen almost right after you've finished eating. That's 'cause cleanup is a breeze!

Since many of these recipes are for large roasts that need to be carved, it's time to sharpen your knives—and your appetites—so we can find out how these bakes and roasts are the answer to mealtime worries:

- Always spray roasting pans with nonstick vegetable spray to keep cleanup easy. Or you can line your roasting pans and baking dishes with aluminum foil.

- When making meat loaf, you can line your pan with either aluminum foil or, believe it or not, waxed paper. Either one will help you remove the loaf from the pan in one piece.

- Let a roast "rest" for 10 to 15 minutes after it comes out of the oven. It will carve more easily, plus it'll be a lot more juicy.

Roasting Pans and Baking Dishes

Oven-to-Table Meals

Dressed-up Meat Loaf

6 to 8 servings

Meat loaf again? You bet . . . but this time you practically won't recognize it. That's 'cause it's teamed with ranch-seasoned potatoes, veggies, and a saucy topping. It's an all-new version of the American classic.

¼ cup olive oil
2 envelopes (1 ounce each) dry ranch dressing mix, divided
6 large potatoes, peeled
6 medium-sized carrots, peeled
1 cup sour cream
2 pounds ground beef
1 pound ground pork
½ cup plain dry bread crumbs
1 egg
¼ cup ketchup

Preheat the oven to 375°F. In a large roasting pan, combine the oil and half an envelope of ranch dressing. Add the potatoes and carrots and toss until thoroughly coated; set aside. In a large bowl, combine the sour cream and the remaining 1½ envelopes ranch dressing. Add the beef, pork, bread crumbs, and egg; mix well. Push the vegetables to the side of the roasting pan and form the meat mixture into an oval loaf in the center of the pan. Spread the ketchup evenly over the meat loaf and cover tightly with aluminum foil. Bake for 1 hour, then uncover and bake for 20 to 30 more minutes, or until the juices from the meat loaf run clear and the potatoes are tender.

Complete Roast Beef Dinner

4 to 6 servings

Let your oven do all the work while you sit back and enjoy hearing all the "ooh"s and "aah"s.

3 cups warm prepared mashed potatoes

2 cans (15 ounces each) mixed vegetables, drained

12 thick slices deli roast beef (about 2 pounds)

1 jar (18 ounces) brown gravy

Preheat the oven to 375°F. In a large bowl, combine the mashed potatoes and vegetables. Place ⅓ cup of the potato mixture at a narrow end of each slice of roast beef and roll up crepe-style. Place the beef rolls seam side down in a large shallow roasting pan, making two rows of six. Pour the gravy over the beef rolls. Cover tightly with aluminum foil and bake for 45 to 50 minutes, or until the rolls are warmed through and the gravy is bubbly.

NOTE: This recipe's great for using leftover mashed potatoes (just warm them in the microwave first), but you can also use instant mashed potatoes prepared according to the package directions.

Mediterranean Veal

4 servings

No fancy preparations needed here! But these veal steaks will tantalize the taste buds with the flavors of garlic, oregano, thyme, and white wine. It's just what I like—easy elegance for everyday eating.

2 veal shoulder steaks (about 2 pounds total)
2 small onions, quartered
6 small red potatoes, cut in half
1 garlic clove, minced
¼ teaspoon dried oregano
¼ teaspoon dried thyme
1 teaspoon salt
½ teaspoon black pepper
¼ cup dry white wine
1 large red bell pepper, cut into 1-inch chunks

Preheat the oven to 325°F. Place the steaks in a 9" × 13" baking dish, then place the onions around them. Top the steaks and onions with the potatoes. Sprinkle with the garlic, oregano, thyme, salt, and black pepper. Pour the wine over the top, cover with aluminum foil, and bake for 45 minutes. Carefully remove the foil and add the bell pepper chunks; recover and bake for 40 to 45 minutes, or until the veal is fork-tender.

Roast Veal Florentine

4 to 6 servings

It sounds fancy. It tastes elegant. But the cost? Really low! (So how could you go wrong?)

½ cup instant mashed potato flakes

¼ cup hot water

3 eggs

1¼ teaspoons salt, divided

2 pounds ground veal

1 package (9 ounces) frozen creamed spinach, thawed

1 cup plain dry bread crumbs

1 teaspoon garlic powder

½ teaspoon black pepper

1 tablespoon ketchup

Preheat the oven to 350°F. In a medium-sized bowl, combine the potato flakes, water, 1 egg, and ¼ teaspoon salt; mix well and set aside. In a large bowl, combine the veal, spinach, bread crumbs, the remaining 2 eggs and 1 teaspoon salt, the garlic powder, and pepper; mix well. Place half of the veal mixture in a 5" × 9" loaf pan that has been coated with nonstick vegetable spray. Pat down the mixture, making a ½-inch indentation lengthwise down the center of the loaf. Fill the indentation with the potato mixture, then gently top the loaf with the remaining meat mixture, pressing down gently to seal the edges. Spread the ketchup over the top of the loaf and bake for 60 to 65 minutes, or until cooked through and the juices run clear. Drain off the excess liquid and let sit for 5 minutes before slicing and serving.

Crown Roast of Lamb

4 servings

Celebrating a special occasion? It's time to pull out all the stops and treat your guests like royalty. Why not make them a crown roast of lamb, seasoned perfectly and stuffed with fluffy rice? They'll be bowing to *you* after they enjoy your tasty meal.

One 2- to 2½-pound crown roast of lamb
1 tablespoon peanut oil
1½ teaspoons salt, divided
½ teaspoon black pepper
1½ cups cooked rice
¼ pound fresh mushrooms, sliced
¼ teaspoon chopped fresh parsley
2 tablespoons butter, melted

Preheat the oven to 325°F. Place the crown roast in a shallow roasting pan that has been coated with nonstick vegetable spray. In a small bowl, combine the oil, 1 teaspoon salt, and the pepper; mix well. Rub the mixture over the entire roast. In a medium-sized bowl, combine the rice, mushrooms, parsley, butter, and the remaining ½ teaspoon salt; mix well. Fill the cavity of the roast with the rice stuffing. Protect the ends of the rib bones from overbrowning by wrapping each of them in aluminum foil. Roast, uncovered, for 1 to 1½ hours, until a meat thermometer registers 160°F. for medium, or until desired doneness beyond that. Transfer the roast to a serving platter and allow to stand for 15 to 20 minutes before slicing between the bones.

NOTE: You can find a crown roast of lamb at the meat counter, or ask the butcher to prepare it for you. Before serving, be sure to discard any string that may have been used by the butcher to tie the roast.

Almost-Stuffed Pork Chops

4 servings

Once you start eating these, you may not be able to stop. So be careful, or the pork chops won't be the only thing getting stuffed!

4 pork loin chops (1¼ to 1½ pounds total), 1 inch thick
Juice of 1 lime (about 2 tablespoons)
1⅓ cups coarsely crumbled cracker crumbs (about 4 ounces crackers)
6 ounces fresh mushrooms, finely chopped (about 1 cup)
3 scallions, chopped
1 tablespoon Dijon-style mustard
1 tablespoon dried parsley flakes

Preheat the oven to 350°F. Brush both sides of the pork chops with the lime juice and lay them in a 9" × 13" baking dish that has been coated with nonstick vegetable spray. In a medium-sized bowl, combine the remaining ingredients. Mix until well blended and spoon evenly over the chops. Bake for 40 to 45 minutes, or until cooked through.

Hoagie Lasagna

4 to 6 servings

I love deli meats like salami, ham, roast beef . . . you name it! And as sandwich makers, they're great. But for a change, we can use them in our lasagna for a one-of-a-kind main course dish.

1 container (32 ounces) ricotta cheese
2 eggs
¼ cup grated Parmesan cheese
1 jar (26 ounces) spaghetti sauce
¾ cup water
¼ pound salami, diced
½ pound deli ham, diced
9 uncooked lasagna noodles
3 cups (12 ounces) shredded mozzarella cheese

Preheat the oven to 350°F. In a medium-sized bowl, combine the ricotta cheese, eggs, and Parmesan cheese. In another medium-sized bowl, combine the spaghetti sauce and water. Spread 1½ cups of the sauce mixture in the bottom of a 9" × 13" baking dish that has been coated with nonstick vegetable spray. Stir the diced meats into the remaining spaghetti sauce mixture. Place 3 lasagna noodles over the sauce in the baking dish, then top with one third of the ricotta cheese mixture. Spoon one third of the remaining sauce mixture over the top, then sprinkle with ¾ cup shredded mozzarella cheese. Repeat the layers 2 more times, starting with noodles, and top with the remaining ¾ cup mozzarella cheese. Cover tightly with aluminum foil and bake for 1½ hours. Remove the foil and bake for 5 more minutes, or until hot and bubbly.

NOTE: Any of your favorite deli meats can be diced and used instead of the salami and ham. Just remember, if you use salty meats, the lasagna will be salty, too.

Cheesy Stuffed Shells

4 to 6 servings

Big shells, big taste, and big "easy," too!

5 cups spaghetti sauce

15 to 18 frozen stuffed shells (about 2½ pounds), thawed

1 package (7 ounces) frozen brown and serve sausages, thawed and thinly sliced

1 cup (4 ounces) shredded Italian cheese blend

Preheat the oven to 350°F. Spread 2 cups of the spaghetti sauce evenly over the bottom of a 9" × 13" baking dish that has been coated with nonstick vegetable spray. Place the stuffed shells in a single layer over the sauce. In a large bowl, combine the sausage and the remaining 3 cups spaghetti sauce. Pour over the shells, completely covering them. Sprinkle the cheese evenly over the top, then cover tightly with aluminum foil and bake for 55 to 60 minutes, or until heated through and bubbly.

NOTE: Five cups of spaghetti sauce is about one and a half 26-ounce jars.

Holiday Turkey Roll-ups

6 servings

A down-home turkey dinner with all the fixin's, prepared in a matter of minutes—in one dish! Now that's the way to celebrate a holiday.

1 package (8 ounces) corn
bread stuffing mix
1 cup water
⅓ cup butter, melted
½ cup sweetened dried
cranberries

1 can (8¾ ounces) whole
kernel corn, drained
12 thick slices deli turkey
(about 2 pounds)
1 jar (12 ounces) turkey gravy

Preheat the oven to 375°F. In a medium-sized bowl, combine the stuffing mix, water, butter, cranberries, and corn; mix well. Place ¼ cup of the stuffing mixture at a narrow end of each slice of turkey and roll up crepe-style. Place the turkey rolls seam-side down, forming two rows of six rolls, in a 9" × 13" baking dish that has been coated with nonstick vegetable spray. Spoon the gravy over the turkey rolls, then cover tightly with aluminum foil. Bake for 35 to 40 minutes, or until heated through.

NOTE: Make sure to ask the deli to slice the turkey thick, so that there are about 6 slices to the pound.

Stuffed Turkey Roll-ups

6 servings

Told ya that turkey isn't only for Thanksgiving and Christmas. Here's year-round proof!

½ cup dry white wine
1 can (10¾ ounces) condensed
    cream of asparagus soup
6 turkey breast cutlets (about
    1 pound total)
1 package (9 ounces) frozen
    asparagus cuts, thawed

2 cups (8 ounces) shredded
    Italian cheese blend
2 cups herb-seasoned
    stuffing mix
½ cup (1 stick) butter, melted

Preheat the oven to 350°F. Pour the wine into a 9" × 13" baking dish that has been coated with nonstick vegetable spray. Add the soup; mix well. Place the turkey in the dish in a single layer, then sprinkle the asparagus cuts evenly over the turkey. Cover with the cheese, then the stuffing mix. Drizzle the butter over the top and bake for 40 to 45 minutes, or until no pink remains in the turkey.

NOTE: If turkey breast cutlets aren't available, it's fine to substitute large chicken cutlets.

Asian Chicken Supreme

4 to 6 servings

I can't decide if it's the ramen noodles, the crunchy veggies, the tender chicken, or the fact that it's a tasty meal-in-one that makes this such a treat! What do you think?

2 packages (3 ounces each)
   ramen noodles, broken up
2 cans (10¾ ounces each)
   condensed cream of
   chicken and broccoli soup
1 cup water
½ cup dry white wine
1 package (16 ounces) frozen
   stir-fry vegetables
   (broccoli, carrots, and
   water chestnuts), thawed

2 packages (9 ounces each)
   frozen cooked breaded
   chicken breast fillets,
   thawed
¼ cup grated Parmesan cheese

Preheat the oven to 350°F. Spread the ramen noodles evenly in the bottom of a 9" × 13" baking dish that has been coated with nonstick vegetable spray (reserve the seasoning packets for another use). In a large bowl, combine the soup, water, and wine. Pour half of the mixture over the noodles, covering them completely. Scatter the vegetables over the soup and noodles. Pour half of the remaining soup mixture over the vegetables. Place the chicken on top and cover with the remaining soup mixture. Sprinkle with the Parmesan cheese and cover tightly with aluminum foil. Bake for 1 hour. Remove the foil and bake for 10 more minutes, or until the top is golden.

Lemon Rosemary Chicken

4 to 6 servings

Lots of colorful veggies, lots of lemon, lots of lip-smacking flavor . . .

½ cup vegetable oil
Juice of 1 lemon
1 tablespoon dried rosemary
1 teaspoon garlic powder
2 teaspoons salt
1½ teaspoons black pepper
One 6½- to 7-pound roasting
   chicken
3 medium-sized yellow
   squash, cut into ½-inch
   slices

3 medium-sized carrots, cut
   into 1-inch slices
2 medium-sized zucchini, cut
   into ½-inch slices
10 small red potatoes, cut into
   quarters

Preheat the oven to 350°F. In a large bowl, combine the oil, lemon juice, rosemary, garlic powder, salt, and pepper; mix well. Place the chicken on a rack in a large roasting pan. Rub half of the seasoning mixture evenly over the whole chicken, inside and out. Place the vegetables and potatoes in the bowl with the remaining seasoning mixture and toss to coat well. Place the vegetables around the chicken in the roasting pan. Cover tightly with aluminum foil and bake for 1½ hours, basting the chicken and vegetables occasionally with the pan juices. Remove the aluminum foil and bake for 25 to 30 more minutes, until the juices run clear and the skin is golden brown.

NOTE: If your chicken is much larger or smaller than 6½ to 7 pounds, you'll have to adjust the cooking time accordingly.

Corn 'n' Chicken Bake

4 servings

Okay, it's time we served something really corny. It's chicken and stuffing packed with the fresh-picked flavor of buttery sweet corn in every bite.

4 boneless, skinless chicken
    breast halves (1 to 1½
    pounds total)
¼ teaspoon garlic powder
½ teaspoon salt
¼ teaspoon black pepper
1 package (8 ounces) corn
    bread stuffing mix
1 can (8¾ ounces) whole
    kernel corn, drained

1 cup boiling water
¼ cup (½ stick) butter, melted
1 can (10¾ ounces) condensed
    golden corn soup
⅓ cup milk
1 tablespoon chopped fresh
    parsley

Preheat the oven to 375°F. Place the chicken breast halves in a single layer in a 7" × 11" baking dish that has been coated with nonstick vegetable spray. Sprinkle with the garlic powder, salt, and pepper. In a large bowl, combine the stuffing mix, corn, water, and butter; mix well. Spoon the stuffing mixture over the chicken. In the same bowl, combine the soup, milk, and parsley; mix well. Pour over the stuffing, then cover with aluminum foil and bake for 35 minutes. Uncover and bake for 5 to 10 more minutes, or until no pink remains in the chicken and the stuffing is golden.

Chicken 'n' Rice

4 to 6 servings

There's a tasty duo in our kitchen that we can always count on . . . and now it's tastier than ever.

1 can (10¾ ounces) condensed
    cream of celery soup
2 cups water
1 cup uncooked long-grain
    parboiled white rice
    (see Note)
1 can (4 ounces) sliced
    mushrooms, drained

2 scallions, thinly sliced
½ teaspoon black pepper
4 chicken leg-thigh quarters,
    cut in half and skin
    removed (see Note)
1 envelope (1 ounce) dry
    onion soup mix

Preheat the oven to 350°F. In a 9" × 13" baking dish, combine the cream of celery soup, water, rice, mushrooms, scallions, and pepper; mix well. Place the chicken on the soup mixture and sprinkle with the onion soup mix. Cover and bake for 65 to 70 minutes, or until no pink remains in the chicken and the juices run clear.

NOTE: Long-grain parboiled white rice, also known as Converted rice, can usually be found in the supermarket rice section. A cut-up whole chicken, chicken thighs, legs, or even chicken breasts can be used here—whatever is your favorite part.

Flounder Oscar

6 servings

In show business, when a movie is top-notch, it wins an Oscar®. And when I really want to make an impression at the dinner table, I make this combo. Wait'll they taste the yummy crabmeat and asparagus filling! It won't be just the fancy name that'll have them applauding.

3 tablespoons butter, cut into small pieces

3 cups frozen shredded hash brown potatoes, thawed

6 flounder fillets (1½ to 2 pounds total)

2 cans (6 ounces each) crabmeat, rinsed, drained, and flaked (see Note)

1 can (10¾ ounces) condensed Cheddar cheese soup

1 package (10 ounces) frozen asparagus spears, thawed and drained

6 slices (6 ounces total) Cheddar cheese

Preheat the oven to 400°F. Place the butter and potatoes in a 9" × 13" baking dish that has been coated with nonstick vegetable spray. Bake for 10 minutes. Meanwhile, place the fish on a baking sheet. In a medium-sized bowl, combine the crabmeat and soup; mix well. Spread the mixture equally over the fish fillets, then top with the asparagus spears and roll up from a short end. With a spoon, push the potatoes to the edges of the baking dish. Place the rolled fillets seam side down in the center of the dish and top each with a slice of cheese. Bake, uncovered, for 30 to 35 minutes, or until the potatoes are golden and the fish flakes easily with a fork.

NOTE: You don't need to pay for higher-priced real crabmeat if you'd rather use imitation. Whichever you use in this will get you plenty of "ooh"s and "aah"s.

The Baking Sheet

Flat-out Favorites

All right, I misled you. When you saw the title of this book, you probably thought of a deep pot simmering all day on the stove . . . or at least a casserole dish full of ingredients bubbling and melting together in the oven. Well, I found a lot of one-pan dishes that work well on baking sheets or pizza pans. And, no, I'm not talking about dishes like beef stew!

When you look through this chapter, you're going to find a load of recipes that are bound to become your family's . . . I have to say it . . . flat-out favorites. When making these:

- Be sure to use a rimmed baking sheet so that any juices or liquid won't drip into the oven.

- Use a sturdy baking sheet that won't twist or warp at high oven temperatures.

- No pizza pan? No problem. Simply make a rectangular pizza on a standard baking sheet.

- I recommend removing pizza from its pan and placing it on a cutting board for cutting instead of cutting it right on the pan. That way, you won't cut through your pans; over time, food will stick to those nicked surfaces and you'll end up ruining the pans.

- If you're making a double batch of a recipe and need to cook two pans at once, place each pan on its own oven shelf, rather than beside each other. This will allow the heat to circulate more evenly in the oven.

The Baking Sheet

Flat-out Favorites

Italian Pesto Shish Kebab

4 servings

A work of art without a lot of work! That pesto sauce you thought you'd use only on pasta makes the difference between dull and daring on these veggie and beef kebabs. It's the taste of the unexpected that gets 'em every time!

1 bottle (8 ounces) Italian
   dressing
1 container (7 ounces) pesto
   sauce
2½ pounds beef tenderloin,
   cut into 24 chunks
1 large red bell pepper, cut
   into 16 pieces

1 can (15 ounces) whole
   potatoes, drained
1 medium-sized zucchini, cut
   into 16 chunks
1 large onion, cut into
   8 wedges

8 metal or wooden skewers

If using wooden skewers, soak them in water for 20 minutes. In a small bowl, combine the Italian dressing and pesto. Thread each skewer with a chunk of beef, then a piece of red pepper, a potato, a chunk of zucchini, another beef chunk, a piece of red pepper, an onion wedge, a chunk of zucchini, and another beef chunk. Place the skewers in a 9" × 13" baking dish and pour the pesto mixture over them. Cover and refrigerate for at least 4 hours, or overnight, turning occasionally. Preheat the broiler. Place the skewers on a broiler pan or rimmed baking sheet that has been coated with nonstick vegetable spray, reserving the marinade. Broil for 8 to 10 minutes, then turn and baste with the reserved marinade. Broil for 6 to 8 more minutes, or until the beef is cooked to the desired doneness. Discard the remaining marinade.

Sun-dried Tomato and Bacon Pizza

2 to 4 servings

No matter how you fancy it up, you can always count on pizza being easy as pie—and a great value, too. This one's a great example of how you can dress up a pizza for just pennies per yummy serving.

1 pound store-bought pizza dough
½ cup pizza or spaghetti sauce
½ cup oil-packed sun-dried tomatoes, drained and cut into thin strips
3 garlic cloves, minced
1 can (3 ounces) real bacon bits

¼ pound fresh mushrooms, sliced
½ cup (2 ounces) crumbled feta cheese
1 cup (4 ounces) shredded mozzarella cheese

Preheat the oven to 450°F. Using your fingertips or the heel of your hand, spread the dough to cover the bottom of a 12- to 14-inch pizza pan that has been coated with nonstick vegetable spray. Push the dough up to the edge of the pan, forming a rim. If the dough is too sticky, dust it and your hands lightly with flour. With a fork, prick the dough 15 to 20 times. Spread the sauce evenly over the dough. Top with the sun-dried tomatoes, garlic, bacon bits, mushrooms, and feta and mozzarella cheeses. Bake for 10 to 14 minutes, or until the crust is crisp and browned.

NOTE: If you prefer to use a prepared 12- to 14-inch pizza shell instead of starting with pizza dough, just reduce the baking time by 3 to 4 minutes.

Turkey Club Pizzazz

6 to 8 slices

What do we get when we add some "z"s to pizza? We get pizzazz. And turkey, bacon, and Cheddar cheese are just the right way to do it!

One 12- to 14-inch prepared
    pizza shell, thawed if
    frozen
1 cup (4 ounces) shredded
    Cheddar cheese

½ pound sliced deli turkey,
    coarsely chopped
¼ cup real bacon bits
2 cups shredded iceberg lettuce
1 medium-sized tomato,
    chopped

Preheat the oven to 450°F. Place the pizza shell on a pizza pan and sprinkle evenly with the cheese. Top with the turkey and sprinkle with the bacon bits. Bake for 10 to 12 minutes, or until the crust is crisp and brown. Top with the shredded lettuce and chopped tomato, cut, and serve.

Meatball Calzones

2 to 4 servings

When you can't decide if you want a sandwich or pizza, have both! These hot and hearty calzones have it all.

1 pound store-bought pizza
 dough
1 package (20 ounces) frozen
 meatballs, thawed
1 can (4 ounces) mushroom
 pieces and stems, drained

½ cup spaghetti sauce
½ cup (2 ounces) shredded
 Italian cheese blend
2 teaspoons olive oil

Preheat the oven to 450°F. Divide the dough into 2 balls. On a lightly floured surface, spread each dough ball with your fingertips or the heel of your hand into a 7- to 8-inch circle. Place half of the meatballs on each dough circle, forming a semicircle on half of each circle and leaving a ½-inch border around the edge. Top the meatballs with the mushrooms, spaghetti sauce, and cheese. Fold the dough over the filling, forming half-moons. With your fingers or a fork, pinch the edges together firmly to seal. Place the calzones on a baking sheet that has been coated with nonstick vegetable spray and brush the top of each with 1 teaspoon oil. Pierce the tops 3 or 4 times with a fork or sharp knife. Bake for 18 to 22 minutes, or until golden brown. Serve whole or cut as desired.

Vegetable Pockets

2 to 4 servings

Flaky baked pockets of garden-fresh veggies and melted cheese are hard to resist. With some warm tomato sauce on the side for dipping, you've got a winning lunch or snack.

1 pound store-bought pizza dough

1 can (4 ounces) whole peeled chilies, drained (see Note)

1 jar (12 ounces) roasted red peppers, drained

1 can (8 ounces) mushroom stems and pieces, drained

½ cup (2 ounces) shredded Italian cheese blend

½ cup canned French-fried onion rings

2 teaspoons olive oil

Preheat the oven to 450°F. Divide the dough into 2 balls. On a lightly floured surface, spread each dough ball with your fingertips or the heel of your hand into a 7- to 8-inch circle. Place half of the chilies, red peppers, and mushrooms on each dough circle, forming a semicircle of filling on half of each circle and leaving a ½-inch border around the edge. Top the filling with the cheese and onion rings. Fold the dough over the filling, forming half-moons. With your fingers or a fork, pinch the edges together firmly to seal. Place the pockets on a baking sheet that has been coated with nonstick vegetable spray and brush the top of each with 1 teaspoon oil. Pierce the tops 3 or 4 times with a fork or sharp knife. Bake for 18 to 22 minutes, or until golden brown. Serve whole or cut as desired.

NOTE: Canned whole chilies can usually be found in the international section of the supermarket, with the Mexican foods.

Pepperoni Mushroom Calzones

2 to 4 servings

Did you know that pepperoni is the number one pizza topping choice? That's why I'd bet it's gonna be your number one calzone filling choice!

1 package (3 ounces) sliced
    pepperoni
1 can (4 ounces) mushroom
    stems and pieces, drained
1 cup (4 ounces) shredded
    mozzarella cheese

⅓ cup spaghetti sauce
1 pound store-bought pizza
    dough
2 teaspoons vegetable oil

Preheat the oven to 450°F. In a medium-sized bowl, combine the pepperoni, mushrooms, cheese, and spaghetti sauce; mix well and set aside. Divide the dough into 2 balls. On a lightly floured surface, spread each dough ball with your fingertips or the heel of your hand into a 7- to 8-inch circle. Spread half of the pepperoni mixture over each dough circle, forming a semicircle of filling on half of each circle and leaving a ½-inch border around the edge. Fold the dough over the filling, forming half-moons. With your fingers or a fork, pinch the edges together firmly to seal. Place the calzones on a baking sheet that has been coated with nonstick vegetable spray and brush the top of each with 1 teaspoon oil. Pierce the tops 3 or 4 times with a fork or sharp knife. Bake for 18 to 22 minutes, or until golden brown. Serve whole or cut as desired.

R & R Chicken Turnovers

4 servings

Four ingredients are all you'll need to turn out herb-flavored home-baked chicken turnovers so fast there'll be loads of time left over for R & R (rest and relaxation)!

1 package (17½ ounces) frozen puff pastry sheets, thawed

1 package (6½ ounces) herb-flavored soft-spread cheese (see Note)

1 can (10 ounces) chunk white chicken, drained and flaked

1 package (9 ounces) frozen French-cut string beans, thawed and drained

Preheat the oven to 400°F. Place the puff pastry on a large cutting board and cut each sheet in half diagonally, yielding a total of 4 large triangles. Spread the cheese evenly over each piece of pastry, leaving a ½-inch border around the edges. Divide the chicken into 4 portions, and place one portion on half of each triangle. Top with equal amounts of the string beans, moisten the edges of the pastry with water, then fold the other half of the triangle over the filling and crimp with your fingers or a fork to seal. Place the turnovers on 2 large rimmed baking sheets that have been coated with nonstick vegetable spray; bake for 20 to 25 minutes, or until golden brown.

NOTE: Soft-spread cheese is usually found in the supermarket refrigerator case near the cream cheese.

Oven-Baked Reubens

4 servings

Love hot stuffed deli sandwiches? How 'bout trying an oven-baked version at home? They're so filling that each one makes a whole meal!

8 slices rye or pumpernickel bread
½ cup Thousand Island dressing
1 pound sliced deli corned beef

1 can (27 ounces) sauerkraut, well drained
8 long slices (12 ounces total) Swiss cheese

Preheat the oven to 350°F. Place the slices of bread on 2 baking sheets that have been covered with aluminum foil. Spread the dressing evenly over the bread. Divide the corned beef evenly over 4 slices of bread. Divide the sauerkraut evenly over the remaining 4 slices of bread. Place a slice of Swiss cheese over each piece of bread and bake for 8 to 10 minutes, or until the cheese is melted and the corned beef is hot. Carefully invert a sauerkraut slice on top of each corned beef slice and cut in half. Serve immediately.

Roasted Vegetable Sandwich

3 to 4 servings

It's so important to "eat our veggies." And when they're served up tender and seasoned on crusty French bread, they're so scrumptious that we can't get enough of them!

1 medium-sized eggplant, peeled and cut into ¼-inch slices
1 medium-sized red onion, cut into ½-inch slices
1 medium-sized red bell pepper, cut into 8 strips
6 garlic cloves, minced
½ cup olive oil
½ teaspoon dried oregano
½ teaspoon dried thyme
½ teaspoon salt
¼ teaspoon black pepper
1 cup (4 ounces) shredded mozzarella cheese
1 loaf (10 ounces) French bread, split in half lengthwise

Preheat the oven to 450°F. In a large roasting pan or rimmed baking sheet, combine all the ingredients except the cheese and bread; toss until well combined. Roast for 35 to 40 minutes, or until the vegetables are tender. Sprinkle with the cheese and bake for 3 to 4 more minutes, or until the cheese melts. Spread evenly over the cut sides of the French bread, then cut and serve immediately.

Bountiful Beef Melt

4 to 6 servings

Talk about a big sandwich. . . . This one's big on size *and* big on taste. Why, there's enough here to feed the whole gang!

1 loaf (1 pound) Italian bread, split in half lengthwise
½ cup garlic butter (see Note)
6 slices (6 ounces total) provolone cheese

1 pound thinly sliced deli roast beef
2 large tomatoes, cut into ½-inch slices

Preheat the oven to 350°F. Spread the cut sides of the bread equally with the garlic butter. Place 3 slices of provolone cheese over the bottom half of the loaf, then alternately layer with the roast beef and tomatoes. Cover with the remaining 3 slices of provolone cheese and replace the top of the bread. Wrap tightly with aluminum foil and bake for 1 hour, or until heated through and the cheese is melted. Unwrap and slice with a serrated knife. Serve immediately.

NOTE: You can buy garlic butter in the refrigerated section of your supermarket, or make your own by adding chopped garlic or garlic powder to taste to softened butter.

Index

Index

185

Index

186

Index

Index

188

Index

Index

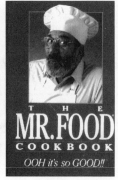

A

B

C

D

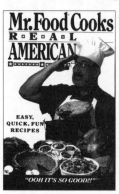
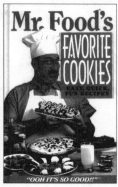

E

F

G

H

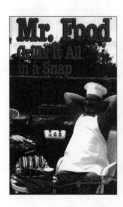

I

J

K

L

Mr. Food®'s Library Gives You More Ways to Say... "OOH IT'S SO GOOD!!®"

WILLIAM MORROW

M

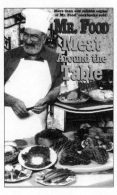

N

O

P

Q

R

S

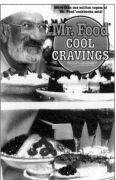

T

Mr. Food ®

Can Help You Be A Kitchen Hero!

Let Mr. Food® make your life easier with
Quick, No-Fuss Recipes and Helpful Kitchen Tips for

Family Dinners • Soups and Salads • Potluck Dishes • Barbecues • Special Brunches • Unbelievable Desserts

... and that's just the beginning!

Complete your Mr. Food® cookbook library today.
It's so simple to share in all the "OOH IT'S SO GOOD!!®"

✂ -

TITLE	PRICE	QUANTITY	
A. Mr. Food® Cooks Like Mama	@ $12.95 each	x _____	= $_____
B. The Mr. Food® Cookbook, OOH IT'S SO GOOD!!®	@ $12.95 each	x _____	= $_____
C. Mr. Food® Cooks Chicken	@ $ 9.95 each	x _____	= $_____
D. Mr. Food® Cooks Pasta	@ $ 9.95 each	x _____	= $_____
E. Mr. Food® Makes Dessert	@ $ 9.95 each	x _____	= $_____
F. Mr. Food® Cooks Real American	@ $14.95 each	x _____	= $_____
G. Mr. Food®'s Favorite Cookies	@ $11.95 each	x _____	= $_____
H. Mr. Food®'s Quick and Easy Side Dishes	@ $11.95 each	x _____	= $_____
I. Mr. Food® Grills It All in a Snap	@ $11.95 each	x _____	= $_____
J. Mr. Food®'s Fun Kitchen Tips and Shortcuts (and Recipes, Too!)	@ $11.95 each	x _____	= $_____
K. Mr. Food®'s Old World Cooking Made Easy	@ $14.95 each	x _____	= $_____
L. "Help, Mr. Food®! Company's Coming!"	@ $14.95 each	x _____	= $_____
M. Mr. Food® Pizza 1-2-3	@ $12.00 each	x _____	= $_____
N. Mr. Food® Meat Around the Table	@ $12.00 each	x _____	= $_____
O. Mr. Food® Simply Chocolate	@ $12.00 each	x _____	= $_____
P. Mr. Food® A Little Lighter	@ $14.95 each	x _____	= $_____
Q. Mr. Food® From My Kitchen to Yours: Stories and Recipes from Home	@ $14.95 each	x _____	= $_____
R. Mr. Food® Easy Tex-Mex	@ $11.95 each	x _____	= $_____
S. Mr. Food® One Pot, One Meal	@ $11.95 each	x _____	= $_____
T. Mr. Food® Cool Cravings	@ $11.95 each	x _____	= $_____

Send payment to:
Mr. Food®
P.O. Box 9227
Coral Springs, FL 33075-9227

Name _____

Street _____ Apt._____

City _____ State_____ Zip_____

Method of Payment: ☐ Check or Money Order Enclosed

☐ Credit Card: ☐ Visa ☐ MasterCard Expiration Date _____

Signature _____

Book Total	$_____
+$2.95 Postage & Handling First Copy **AND** $1 Ea. Add'l. Copy (Canadian Orders Add Add'l. $2.00 *Per Copy*)	$_____
Subtotal	$_____
Less $1.00 per book if ordering 3 or more books with this order	$ – _____
Add Applicable Sales Tax (FL Residents Only)	$_____
Total in U.S. Funds	$_____

Account #: ☐ ☐ ☐ ☐ ☐ ☐ ☐ ☐ ☐ ☐ ☐ ☐ ☐ ☐

Please allow 4 to 6 weeks for delivery.